Vintage
Granny Squares

20 crochet projects with a retro vibe

EMMA VARNAM

THE GUILD OF MASTER CRAFTSMAN PUBLICATIONS

Contents

Introduction

It was a vintage heirloom blanket that caught my attention and drew me into learning to crochet. Firstly, the pattern of the stitches was so mesmerizing, I wanted to know how it was done. Secondly, I realized that the blanket was made up of a myriad of colours. It was a crochet blanket made during or just after the Second World War using recycled jumpers, socks and hats. The fabulous 'make-do-and-mend' generation were at the forefront of re-purposing resources, making something beautiful from something worn or broken. The blanket was full of boring greys, tedious bottle green, a flash of dull red and then a horrible clashing yellow. And yet it looked beautiful.

The genius of vintage crochet is that, like nature, there are no clashes – just creativity. It was my hope that if I could learn to crochet, I could harness this historic superpower and whittle down my growing yarn stash. I wish I could tell you that has happened. If anything, the stash has grown, but so has my love of crochet.

Vintage crochet is a deep well of inspiration. If you look at any book or magazine that celebrates classic British style you will frequently spot a crochet blanket or cushion in vibrant hues. They will be found draped on the back of squishy sofas or used as the base for a cheerful picnic. In this book I have designed patterns which are based around the classic vintage granny square, but have a modern twist.

Many of these projects will not take you long to make. They are quick and easy to complete if you have learnt the basics of crochet. The projects themselves are also intended to be used, relaxing at your leisure.

Throughout the book you will find hints and tips which I hope will improve your crochet technique and are good hobby hacks. I have tried to give you help and knowledge which will allow you to avoid the mistakes I have made over the years.

The beauty of crochet is that it is a wonderfully relaxing hobby; a perfect, practical distraction from the worries of work, study and a busy life. Let your fingers soothe away your concerns as you chat with friends or watch the telly.

Getting Started

What You'll Need

The word 'crochet' means 'hook' in French. Unlike knitting, crochet is worked with just one hook, creating a series of connected loops from yarn.

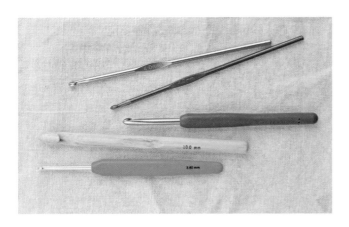

Crochet hooks

Crochet hooks come in a wonderful range of materials and sizes. In this book I've used different sizes according to the thickness of the yarn. For size 3.5mm or 4mm I like to use a metal-pointed ergonomic crochet hook. The larger hooks, such as 8mm or 9mm, are usually made either in plastic or wood.

Yarn

I love working with natural and soft yarns. When I make babywear or clothes for myself, I choose the most expensive yarn I can afford at the time. Pure wool or yarn with a cashmere fibre added to it is very luxurious and soft to the touch. But this type of yarn is for very special projects – heirloom pieces, if you like. Merino wool is ideal for soft scarves or children's garments.

Yarn used for homewear needs to be very hardwearing. These items are likely to get dirty and will benefit from being thrown in the washing machine.

Handy tip

I have given you specific yarn makes and shades for the projects in this book, but really the joy of vintage-style crochet is to use up odds and ends. Start working through that yarn stash to create beautiful items from leftovers. If you want to tie the look of the project together, then choose one colour which creates the edging for the project.

Cotton

Cotton yarn is wonderful for summer wear and accessories for the garden. The colours have a very appealing clarity and brightness. Cotton is also very durable and is less likely to disintegrate with extensive use. Worked in tight, close stitches, cotton forms a very firm fabric, and that is why many toy designers use it as their go-to material.

Acrylic yarns and mixes

Acrylic yarns have improved greatly in the past few years. Once upon a time, they were always a garish colour and were super-scratchy. Recent technology has ensured that acrylic yarn and their blends feel almost as soft as merino or cashmere. They also come in a wide range of subtle and natural colours. It takes a very seasoned eye to tell

the difference. However, the advantage to acrylic yarns is that they are made from ethylene, which is derived from oil. The yarn is robust and resistant to moths and can be washed without worry. Also, it is cheaper to manufacture yarn in this way and so buying enough to make a blanket doesn't have to break the bank.

Needles

You will need a variety of needles for completing the projects, including a tapestry needle for sewing in ends and adding embroidery details, and a fine beading needle for sewing on beads.

Conversions

Crochet hooks		
UK	**Metric**	**US**
14	2mm	–
13	2.25mm	B/1
12	2.5mm	–
–	2.75mm	C/2
11	3mm	–
10	3.25mm	D/3
9	3.5mm	E/4
–	3.75mm	F/5
8	4mm	G/6
7	4.5mm	7
6	5mm	H/8
5	5.5mm	I/9
4	6mm	J/10
3	6.5mm	K/10.5
2	7mm	–
0	8mm	L/11
00	9mm	M–N/13
000	10mm	N–P/15

Crochet Techniques

In this section you can learn the basic techniques. Some will need a bit of practice, but once you have learnt them you can work a number of crochet techniques that are perfect for your vintage projects.

Holding yarn

With the hand you are not using to hold the hook, wrap the yarn around your little finger and then drape the yarn over your hand. You can hold the tail of your yarn between the middle finger and your thumb and use your index finger to control the yarn.

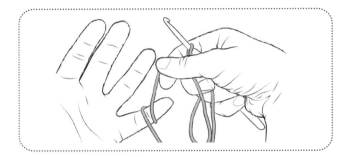

Making a slip knot

Make a loop of yarn over two fingers. Pull a second loop through this first loop, pull it up and slip it onto your crochet hook. Pull the knot gently so that it forms a loose knot on the hook.

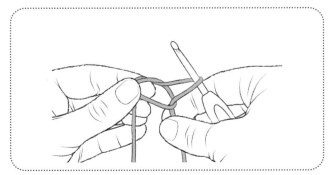

Holding a hook

Hold your hook in either your right or your left hand as you would a pen, in between your index finger and thumb.

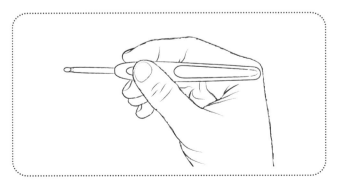

UK and US differences

Some UK and US terms have different meanings, which can cause confusion, so always check which style the pattern you are using is written in. This will ensure that your crochet develops correctly. There is nothing more frustrating than working on a pattern, then realising it is all wrong and needs to be unravelled.

UK/US crochet terms

UK	US
Double crochet	Single crochet
Half treble	Half double crochet
Treble	Double crochet
Double treble	Triple crochet
Treble treble	Double triple crochet

Note: This book use UK crochet terms.

UK/US yarn weights

UK	US
Chunky	Bulky
Aran	Worsted
Double knitting (DK)	Light worsted
4ply	Sport

Abbreviations

alt	alternate
blo	back loop only
bob	bobble
ch	chain
ch sp	chain space
cm	centimetres
cont	continue
dc	double crochet
dc2inc	double crochet increase by one stitch
dc2tog	double crochet two stitches together (decrease by one stitch)
dc3tog	double crochet three stitches together (decrease by two stitches)
dec	decrease
DK	double knitting
dtr	double treble
flo	front loop only
g	grams
htr	half treble
in	inch(es)
inc	increase
lhtr	linked half treble
m	metre(s)
mm	millimetre(s)
rep	repeat
RS	right side
rtrb	raised treble back
rtrf	raised treble front
sl st	slip stitch
sp	space
st(s)	stitch(es)
tbl	through the back loop
tog	together
tr	treble
tr2inc	work 2 tr into same st
tr2tog	treble crochet two stitches together (decrease by one stitch)
WS	wrong side
yd	yard(s)
yo	yarn over

Chain stitch (ch st)

1 Start with a slip knot on the hook.

2 Wrap the yarn over the hook.

3 Pull the loop through the loop of the slip knot to form one chain stitch.

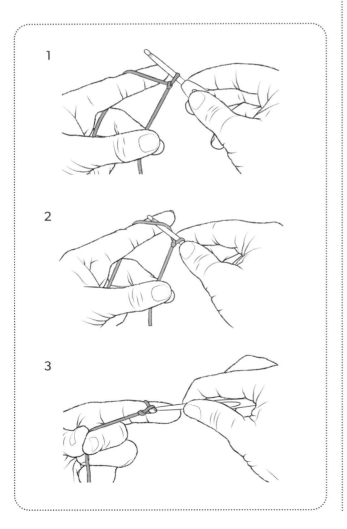

Slip stitch (sl st)

This stitch is ideal for decoration and for attaching two pieces of crochet together.

1 Insert the hook into a stitch and wrap the yarn over the hook.

2 Draw the loop through the stitch and the loop on the hook. Continue in this way for the required number of slip stitches.

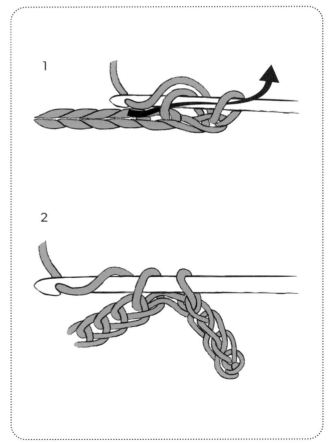

Double crochet (dc)

1 Insert the hook through the stitch, yarn over the hook, and pull through the stitch. There will be two loops on the hook.

2 Wrap the yarn over the hook and pull through both loops on the hook. There will be one loop on the hook.

Half treble (htr)

1 Wrap the yarn over the hook, insert the hook through the stitch, yarn over the hook and pull through the stitch. There will be three loops on the hook.

2 Wrap the yarn over the hook again and draw through all the loops on the hook. There will be one loop on the hook.

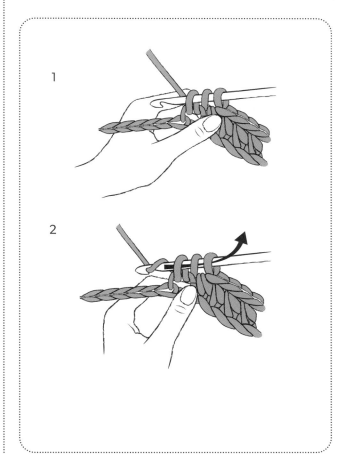

Treble crochet (tr)

1 Wrap the yarn over the hook and insert the hook through the stitch. Wrap the yarn over the hook and pull through the stitch.

2 Wrap the yarn over the hook and pull through two loops. There will be two loops on the hook.

3 Wrap the yarn over the hook again and pull through the remaining two loops. There will be one loop left on the hook.

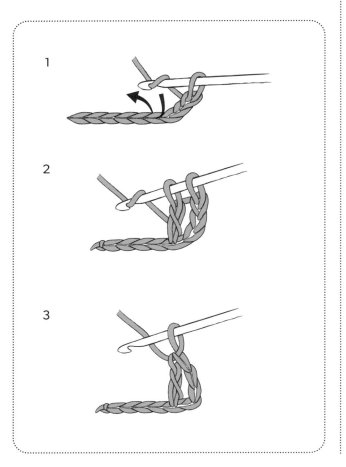

Double treble (dtr)

1 Wrap the yarn over the hook twice, insert the hook through the stitch, yarn over the hook and pull through the stitch. There will be four loops on the hook.

2 Wrap the yarn over the hook and pull through two loops. There will be three loops on the hook.

3 Wrap the yarn over the hook and pull through two loops. There will be two loops on the hook.

4 Wrap the yarn over and pull through the remaining two loops. There will be one loop on the hook.

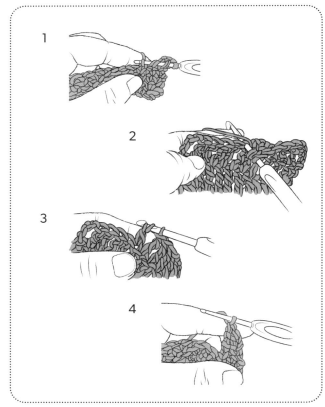

Working in rows

There are not that many patterns in this book that work in rows. However, the tank top uses rows to add a sleeve and the mitten design uses rows to add crochet for the palm. When making straight rows, you need to make a turning chain at the beginning of the row for the stitch you are working on. A double crochet row will need one chain at the beginning of the row; this will be indicated in the pattern.

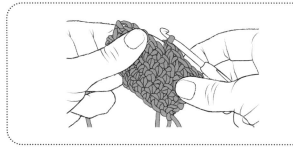

Working in spirals

In some of the patterns in this book you are asked to work in spiral rounds. This means crocheting in a continuous spiral with no slip-stitch joins or turning chains. In this way, you can create one seamless cylindrical shape.

In order to know where each row starts it is advisable to place a marker at the beginning of each row.

Joining a ring

1 Work the number of chain stitches specified in the instructions for your pattern.

2 Insert the hook into the first chain stitch made.

3 Wrap the yarn over the hook and pull through two stitches on the hook.

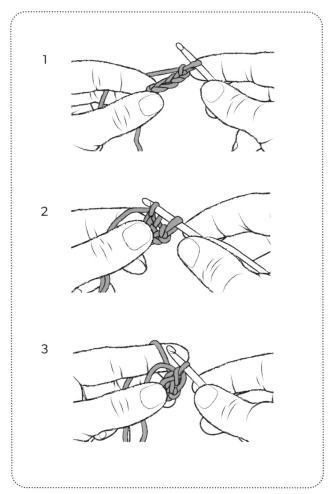

Magic ring

A very clever way to start a seamless shape is to use a 'magic ring'. This is a neat way of starting a circular piece of crochet while avoiding the unsightly hole that can be left in the centre when you join a ring the normal way. Magic rings are nearly always made with double crochet stitches, as this creates a tight, dense fabric.

1 Start by making a basic slip knot. Pull up the loop and slip this loop onto your crochet hook.

2 Before you tighten the ring, wrap the yarn over the hook (outside the circle) and pull through to make the first chain.

3 Insert the hook into the ring, wrap the yarn over the hook and pull through the ring so there are two loops on the hook.

4 Wrap the yarn over the hook again (outside the circle) and pull through both loops.

5 You have made your first double crochet stitch.

6 Continue to work like this for as many double crochet stitches as are stated in the pattern instructions.

7 Pull the yarn tail to tighten the ring and then continue working in the round as usual.

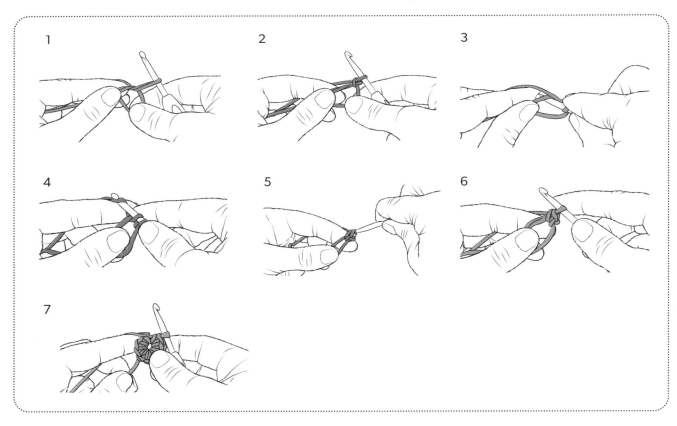

Increasing

Work a stitch as normal, then work another into the same stitch of the previous row.

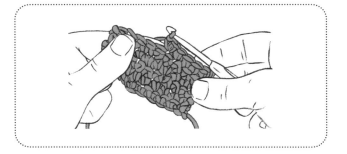

Decreasing (dc2tog)

1 Insert your hook into the next stitch, pull a loop through, insert your hook into the next stitch, and pull a loop through.

2 Wrap the yarn over the hook and pull the yarn through all three loops.

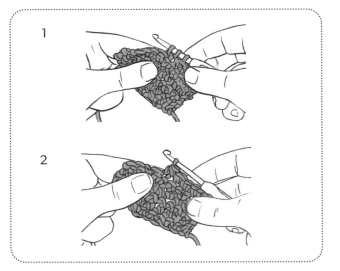

Crocheting into spaces

In some patterns, including classic granny square crochet, you will need to work into a chain space made in the previous row, instead of working into a stitch. When you begin a row with a new colour you join with a slip stitch working into a chain space.

Working in the back loop

Generally, a crochet stitch is made by slipping the hook under the top two loops of a stitch. However, you can also create a different effect by working into the back loop only of each stitch of one round or row. This creates a ridge or horizontal bar across the row.

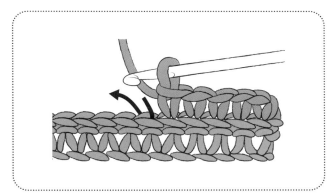

Making granny squares

This is my favourite technique of creating granny squares. I find it helpful when you are making a one-colour square and I like it because it makes it easier to see where the round begins, and my squares appear more regular.

Round 1: Using 4mm hook and first colour, ch 4 sts, join with a sl st to form a ring.

Round 2: Ch 6 (this counts as the first tr and 3 ch), (3 tr into ring, 3 ch) 3 times, 2 tr into ring, sl st into 3rd of 6 ch at the beg of round. Fasten off.

Round 3: Change to second colour. Attach yarn in any corner chain sp using a sl st, 6 ch (counts as the first tr and 3 ch), 3 tr into same ch sp, *1 ch, miss 3 tr, (3 tr, 3 ch, 3 tr) into next ch sp, rep from * twice, 1 ch, miss 3 tr, 2 tr into next ch sp, sl st into 3rd of 6 ch at beg of round. Fasten off.

Round 4: Change to third colour. Attach yarn in any corner chain sp using a sl st, 6 ch (counts as the first tr and 3 ch), 3 tr into same ch sp, *1 ch, miss 3 tr, 3 tr into next ch sp, 1 ch, miss 3 tr, (3 tr, 3 ch, 3 tr) into next ch sp, rep from * twice, 1 ch, miss 3 tr, 3 tr into next ch sp, 1 ch, miss 3 tr, 2 tr into next ch sp, sl st into 3rd of 6 ch at beg of round. Fasten off.

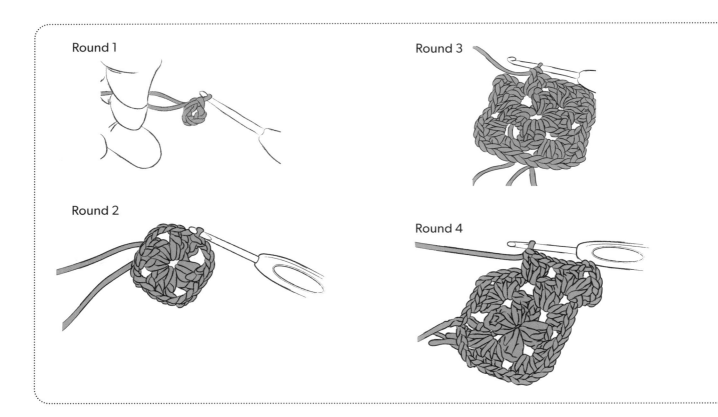

Round 1

Round 2

Round 3

Round 4

Round 5: Change to fourth colour. Attach yarn in any corner chain sp using a sl st, 6 ch (counts as the first tr and 3 ch), 3 tr into same ch sp, *(1 ch, miss 3 tr, 3 tr into next ch sp) twice, 1 ch, miss 3 tr, (3 tr, 3 ch, 3 tr) into next ch sp, rep from * twice, (1 ch, miss 3 tr, 3 tr into next ch sp) twice, 1 ch, miss 3 tr, 2 tr into next ch sp, sl st into 3rd of 6 ch at beg of round. Fasten off.

Keep going like this, changing the colours and increasing the number of treble clusters in each round until you have a very big square. Alternatively, you can make a number of small squares and join them together to make cushions, blankets or even a scarf. One granny square can also make a very quick and easy drinks coaster.

Round 5

Raised treble front (rtrf)

This is a brilliant technique for creating texture and gives a ribbed effect. I have used this technique to edge the shrug. You work your crochet hook around the stitches created on the previous row.

1 Wrap the yarn over the hook and insert your hook from front to back around the post of the next stitch.

2 Wrap the yarn over the hook and pull the yarn through so that you have three loops on your hook. Wrap the yarn over the hook and pull through all three loops.

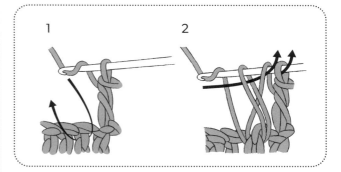

Raised treble back (rtrb)

For rtrb, the method is exactly the same as rtrf (above) except that in step 1 you insert your hook from the back to the front.

Finishing Touches

Whip stitch

You can use whip stitch to sew two layers of fabric together. Make a knot at the end of your yarn. Bring your needle from the wrong side through to the right side of your fabric, then hold both pieces of your fabric together, wrong sides facing each other. Push your needle through the back piece to the front piece, and repeat evenly along the edge. There will be a row of small stitches along the edge of your work, joining both pieces together.

Slip-stitch seam

Place the pieces of the crochet together with wrong sides facing each other. Insert the hook through both pieces at the beginning of the seam and pull up a loop, then chain one stitch. Work a row of slip stitches by inserting your hook through both sides at the same time.

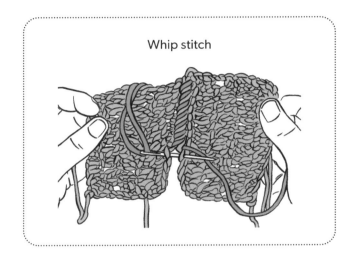

Whip stitch

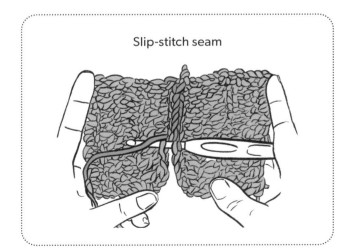

Slip-stitch seam

Double crochet seams

Work as for a slip-stitch seam but working double crochet instead of slip stitch. If you work around a corner, work three small stitches into the corners.

Weaving in ends

Make sure you leave about 8in (20cm) of yarn when you fasten off. You may be able to hide the tail in your next row. I always ensure that my ends have been woven backwards and forwards three times.

1 Thread the remaining yarn end onto a blunt tapestry needle and weave in the yarn on the wrong side of the project. Work along the stitches one way and then work back in the opposite direction.

2 Weave the needle behind the first ridge of crochet for at least 2in (5cm). Snip off the end of the yarn close to the fabric of the crochet.

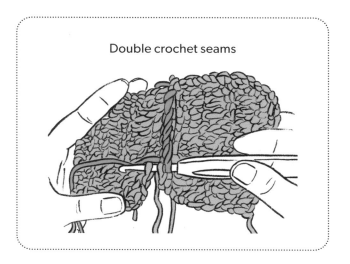

Double crochet seams

Handy tip

Crocheters often dread weaving in ends. My advice is to break up the chore into manageable chunks. For instance, once you have made your first ten squares (for a blanket, say), weave in those ends before you start the next ten squares. This will make the final finishing work far less daunting.

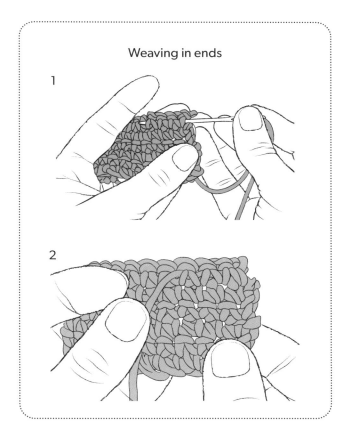

Weaving in ends

1

2

Using a pompom maker

1 Open out the two sections on one side of the pompom maker and wrap your yarn tightly around both pieces. Continue until you have filled the whole side.

2 Repeat on the other side.

3 Close both sides to make a complete circle. With sharp, pointed scissors, cut between the ridges around the edge of the circle.

4 Tie 12in (30cm) of your yarn tightly around the middle of the pompom maker in a secure knot.

5 Carefully pull apart the pompom maker from the centre to release the pompom. Trim the pompom with scissors to make sure it looks even and fluffy.

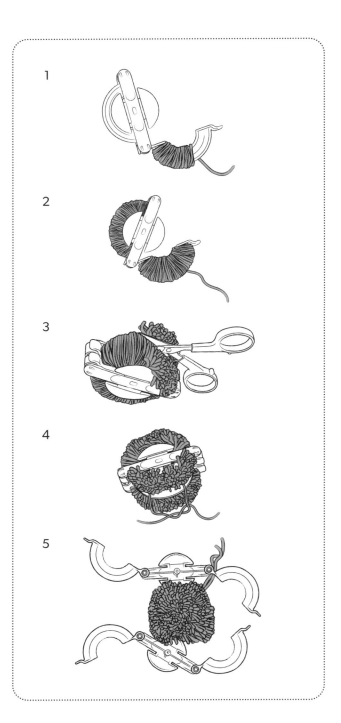

Blocking

One of the most useful techniques you can learn is to 'block' your work into shape once it is finished. Blocking your work can really transform your projects. During the making process, the fibres of the yarn can often become crumpled and creased. By blocking your work, the fibres can relax, and the stitches become regular and even.

When you have finished a mountain of squares, the temptation is to start joining your rows as soon as possible. But if you block each square first, you will find the joining process much simpler. It is easier to see where the edge stitches correspond for joining the seams together. Block the completed project again once you have finished the edging and woven in all the ends.

Lay your project out on an ironing board or a similar surface (flat and padded). Start at one corner and pin gradually along the edges, gently pulling the crochet into place, and secure with a pin. As you work around the edges, you might notice that you have pulled one area more taut than another. Simply remove the pins and reshape. Once you are happy with the overall dimensions, spray the item all over with tepid water. Then leave the crochet to dry completely. Ideally, you should leave your work for two or three days if you can.

Tassels

1 Fold a 4 x 4in (10 x 10cm) piece of card in half and ensure the fold is at the top.

2 Place a 6in (15cm) strand of yarn along the top of the fold, then wrap the yarn 30 times over the cardboard.

3 Knot the strand of yarn firmly along the top of the wrap.

4 Cut the yarn through the open part of the cardboard (at the bottom) and slip the card out.

5 Take another strand of yarn and wrap it 4 times about ½in (1cm) from the top of the knotted end to create the tassel. Secure with a firm knot.

6 Trim the ends of the tassel.

Handy tip

Even experienced crocheters need to check that they have the correct number of stitches or rows. I don't use expensive stitch markers but just cut a small amount of yarn, about 2in (5cm) long, and place this between the last stitch of one row and the first stitch of the next row. When I have finished, these small strands can easily be pulled out without snagging the stitches.

The
Projects

Project Basket

I always have several crochet projects on the go at all times.
I find it helpful to have a number of project baskets that I can
choose from to keep my yarn handy. If they are going to be
seen in and around the house it is worth making them in a variety
of pretty colours. This project is quick to make and would be
an ideal present for any crafting friend.

Finished size

Bag is approximately 9½in (24cm) wide and 11in (28cm) high

You will need

- Stylecraft Special Aran, 100% acrylic (214yd/196m per 100g ball):
  1 x 1246 Lipstick (A)
  1 x 1005 Cream (B)
  1 x 1839 Watermelon (C)
  1 x 1241 Fondant (D)
  1 x 1711 Spice (E)
  1 x 1081 Saffron (F)
  1 x 1832 Mushroom (G)
- 4mm (USG/6:UK8) crochet hook
- Tapestry needle

For the base and lining (optional)
- A 8½ x 8½in (22 x 22cm) square of cardboard
- 5 squares of felt, 9 x 9in (23 x 23cm), for the lining
- Craft glue
- Sewing thread and needle

Tension

This is not essential for this pattern but each square motif is approximately 7 x 7in (18 x 18cm).

Note

It is possible to just crochet the bag, but if you want to create a more stable structure, place a square of cardboard in the base and then line the bag.

Basic square

Round 1: Using 4mm hook and A, ch 4 sts, join with a sl st to form a ring.

Round 2: Ch 6 (this counts as the first tr and 3 ch), (3 tr into ring, 3 ch) 3 times, 2 tr into ring, sl st into 3rd of 6 ch at the beg of round. Fasten off.

Round 3: Attach B in any corner chain sp with a sl st, 6 ch (counts as the first tr and 3 ch), 3 tr into same ch sp, *1 ch, miss 3 tr, (3 tr, 3 ch, 3 tr) into next ch sp; rep from * twice, 1 ch, miss 3 tr, 2 tr into next ch sp, sl st into 3rd of 6 ch at beg of round. Fasten off.

Round 4: Attach C in any corner chain sp with a sl st, 6 ch (counts as the first tr and 3 ch), 3 tr into same ch sp, *1 ch, miss 3 tr, 3 tr into next ch sp, 1 ch, miss 3 tr, (3 tr, 3 ch, 3 tr) into next ch sp; rep from * twice, 1 ch, miss 3 tr, 3 tr into next ch sp, 1 ch, miss 3 tr, 2 tr into next ch sp, sl st into 3rd of 6 ch at beg of round. Fasten off.

Round 5: Attach D in any corner chain sp with a sl st, 6 ch (counts as the first tr and 3 ch), 3 tr into same ch sp, *(1 ch, miss 3 tr, 3 tr into next ch sp) twice, 1 ch, miss 3 tr, (3 tr, 3 ch, 3 tr) into next ch sp; rep from * twice, (1 ch, miss 3 tr, 3 tr into next ch sp) twice, 1 ch, miss 3 tr, 2 tr into next ch sp, sl st into 3rd of 6 ch at beg of round. Fasten off.

Continue increasing the granny square in this manner using the colour sequence: E, B, A, C. Work until you have 32 treble clusters ending with a row in C.

Round 10: Attach B in any corner ch sp with a sl st, 2 ch (counts as the first dc and 1 ch), 1 dc into same ch sp, 1 dc into each tr and 1 dc into every 1 ch, (1 dc, 1 ch, 1 dc) into every 3 ch sp, sl st into 1 ch at beg of round. Fasten off.

Round 11: Attach G in any corner ch sp with a sl st, 2 ch (counts as the first dc and 1 ch), 1 dc into same ch sp, 1 dc into each tr and 1 dc into every 1 ch, (1 dc, 1 ch, 1 dc) into every 1 ch sp, sl st into 1 ch at beg of round. Fasten off and weave in ends.

Make a further 3 squares using the granny square pattern but use the colour sequences.

Square 2: Rounds 1 & 2: C, Round 3: B, Round 4: F, Round 5: A, Round 6: D, Round 7: B, Round 8: A, Round 9: F, Round 10: B, Round 11: G.

Square 3: Rounds 1 & 2: D, Round 3: B, Round 4: G, Round 5: E, Round 6: A, Round 7: B, Round 8: D, Round 9: G, Round 10: B, Round 11: G.

Square 4: Rounds 1 & 2: E, Round 3: B, Round 4: D, Round 5: F, Round 6: C, Round 7: B, Round 8: E, Round 9: D, Round 10: B, Round 11: G.

Base square

(make 1)

Round 1: Using 4mm hook and G, ch 6 sts, join with a sl st to form a ring.

Round 2: Ch 5 (this counts as 1 tr, 2 ch), 3 tr into ring, *2 ch, 3 tr; rep from * twice, 2 ch, 2 tr, sl st into 3rd ch at the beg of round (4 tr clusters). Do not fasten off.

Round 3: Sl st into 2 ch sp, 3 ch (counts as 1 tr), (1 tr, 2 ch, 2 tr) into same ch sp, *1 tr into each tr across side of square, (2 tr, 2 ch, 2 tr) into next 3 ch sp; rep from * twice, 1 tr in each tr across side of square, join with a sl st into 3rd of 3 ch.

Continue to work in rounds expanding the number of each tr stitches until you have worked 9 rounds. Fasten off (124 tr).

Finishing

Weave in all ends. Arrange the granny squares so that there is a square touching each of the four sides of the base. Join the squares to the base by using G and by either sewing the sides together or by crocheting the edges together using a sl st. Join the side seams of the granny squares together to form an open box.

Top edge and handles

Round 1: Using 4mm hook and G, attach yarn to any st along the top edge of the basket, place marker, work 1 dc in each st and 1 dc in the top of any side seam. Keep working in a spiral.

Round 2: 1 dc in each st.

Rounds 3–5: Change to yarn B, 1 dc in each st. Fasten off.

Choose which squares will have the handles; they must be opposite each other. Using some stitch markers mark the centre twenty stitches of the squares.

Round 6: Change to yarn C, work 1 dc in each st until you meet a marker, 20 ch, miss 20 dc, 1 dc in next st with a marker, 1 dc in each stitch until you reach the next handle marker, 20 ch, miss 20 dc, 1 dc in next st with a marker, continue until you have completed rnd.

Round 7: 1 dc in every st and every ch.

Rounds 8–10: 1 dc in every st to end. Fasten off.

Round 11: Change to yarn A, 1 dc in every st to end. Fasten off the end.

Lining

Using some craft glue, cover one side of the square of cardboard, then place in the base of the basket. Leave to dry.

Make a felt lining by arranging the felt squares in the same format as you did for the crochet squares. Sew the base and side seams together. Place inside the basket and sew the top of the lining to the edging using small stitches.

Small Vintage Bag

Granny squares can be sophisticated, and what could be more elegant than a small evening bag in muted tones? The circular resin handles give this design the ultimate vintage look. You can crochet a few bags to go with your favourite outfit, and they make a wonderful gift for a special occasion.

Finished size

8in (20cm) wide and 14in (35.5cm) high with handles

You will need

- Scheepjes Catona 4ply, 100% mercerized cotton (27yd/25m per 10g ball):
  1 x 408 Old Rose (A)
  1 x 105 Bridal White (B)
  1 x 395 Willow (C)
  1 x 406 Soft Beige (D)
  1 x 528 Silver Blue (E)
  1 x 244 Spruce (F)
  2 x 251 Garden Rose (G)
- 3.5mm (US4/E4:UK9) crochet hook
- 5in (13cm) circular resin handles
- Tapestry needle

Tension

This is not essential for this pattern but each square motif is approximately 7½ x 7½in (19 x 19cm).

Note

You will need to make two square motifs for this design. You then slip stitch the two sides and base together. The top of the bag is created working decreasing rows of treble stitch, which you then encase the handles with.

Basic square
(make 2)

Round 1: Using 3.5mm hook and A, ch 4 sts, join with a sl st to form a ring.

Round 2: Ch 6 (this counts as the first tr and 3 ch), (3 tr into ring, 3 ch) 3 times, 2 tr into ring, sl st into 3rd of 6 ch at the beg of round. Fasten off.

Round 3: Attach yarn B in any corner chain sp with a sl st, 6 ch (counts as the first tr and 3 ch), 3 tr into same ch sp, *1 ch, miss 3 tr, (3 tr, 3 ch, 3 tr) into next ch sp; rep from * twice, 1 ch, miss 3 tr, 2 tr into next ch sp, sl st into 3rd of 6 ch at beg of round. Fasten off.

Round 4: Attach yarn C in any corner chain sp with a sl st, 6 ch (counts as the first tr and 3 ch), 3 tr into same ch sp, *1 ch, miss 3 tr, 3 tr into next ch sp, 1 ch, miss 3 tr, (3 tr, 3 ch, 3 tr) into next ch sp; rep from * twice, 1 ch, miss 3 tr, 3 tr into next ch sp, 1 ch, miss 3 tr, 2 tr into next ch sp, sl st into 3rd of 6 ch at beg of round. Fasten off.

Round 5: Attach yarn D in any corner chain sp with a sl st, 6 ch (counts as the first tr and 3 ch), 3 tr into same ch sp, *(1 ch, miss 3 tr, 3 tr into next ch sp) twice, 1 ch, miss 3 tr, (3 tr, 3 ch, 3 tr) into next ch sp; rep from * twice, (1 ch, miss 3 tr, 3 tr into next ch sp) twice, 1 ch, miss 3 tr, 2 tr into next ch sp, sl st into 3rd of 6 ch at beg of round. Fasten off.

Round 6: Attach yarn B in any corner chain sp with a sl st, 6 ch (counts as the first tr and 3 ch), 3 tr into same ch sp, *(1 ch, miss 3 tr, 3 tr into next ch sp) 3 times, 1 ch, miss 3 tr, (3 tr, 3 ch, 3 tr) into next ch sp; rep from * twice, (1 ch, miss 3 tr, 3 tr into next ch sp) 3 times, 1 ch, miss 3 tr, 2 tr into next ch sp, sl st into 3rd of 6 ch at beg of round. Fasten off.

Round 7: Attach yarn A in any corner chain sp with a sl st, 6 ch (counts as the first tr and 3 ch), 3 tr into same ch sp, *(1 ch, miss 3 tr, 3 tr into next ch sp) 4 times, 1 ch, miss 3 tr, (3 tr, 3 ch, 3 tr) into next ch sp; rep from * twice, (1 ch, miss 3 tr, 3 tr into next ch sp) 4 times, 1 ch, miss 3 tr, 2 tr into next ch sp, sl st into 3rd of 6 ch at beg of round. Fasten off.

Round 8: Attach yarn E in any corner chain sp with a sl st, 6 ch (counts as the first tr and 3 ch), 3 tr into same ch sp, *(1 ch, miss 3 tr, 3 tr into next ch sp) 5 times, 1 ch, miss 3 tr, (3 tr, 3 ch, 3 tr) into next ch sp; rep from * twice, (1 ch, miss 3 tr, 3 tr into next ch sp) 5 times, 1 ch, miss 3 tr, 2 tr into next ch sp, sl st into 3rd of 6 ch at beg of round. Fasten off.

Round 9: Attach yarn F in any corner chain sp with a sl st, 6 ch (counts as the first tr and 3 ch), 3 tr into same ch sp, *(1 ch, miss 3 tr, 3 tr into next ch sp) 6 times, 1 ch, miss 3 tr, (3 tr, 3 ch, 3 tr) into next ch sp; rep from * twice, (1 ch, miss 3 tr, 3 tr into next ch sp) 6 times, 1 ch, miss 3 tr, 2 tr into next ch sp, sl st into 3rd of 6 ch at beg of round. Fasten off.

Round 10: Attach yarn G in any corner chain sp with a sl st, 6 ch (counts as the first tr and 3 ch) ,3 tr into same ch sp, *(1 ch, miss 3 tr, 3 tr into next ch sp) 7 times, 1 ch, miss 3 tr, (3 tr, 3 ch, 3 tr) into next ch sp; rep from * twice, (1 ch, miss 3 tr, 3 tr into next ch sp) 7 times, 1 ch, miss 3 tr, 2 tr into next ch sp, sl st into 3rd of 6 ch at beg of round. Do not fasten off.

Handle top
(both squares)

Work along the top of the square.

Row 1: Ch 3, tr2tog in first 2 sts, 1 tr in each st and ch until last 2 sts and corner ch sp, tr3tog, turn.

Rows 2–5: Ch 3, tr2tog in first 2 sts, 1 tr in each st and ch until last 3 sts, tr3tog, turn.

Rows 6–7: Ch 3, 1 tr in each st to end, turn.

Do not fasten off. Leave a long tail of yarn. Fold the last two rows over the circular handle and with WS facing sew to the inside of the treble stitches.

Finishing

Weave in ends and block each of your two squares. With wrong sides facing, using yarn G and a 3.5mm hook, slip stitch (see page 40) the two sides and the base of the squares together. Fasten off and weave in ends.

Cosy Tank Top

I love to wear comfortable hand-crocheted jumpers at the weekend, as they are so warm and cosy. This is quick to make up and the fit is intended to be loose.

Finished size

Tank top is approximately 19½in (50cm) wide and 26in (65cm) long.

You will need

- Stylecraft Special Aran, 100% acrylic (214yd/196m per 100g ball):
  1 x 1854 French Navy (A)
  1 x 1003 Aster (B)
  1 x 1820 Duck Egg (C)
  1 x 1725 Sage (D)
  1 x 1722 Storm Blue (E)
  1 x 1822 Pistachio (F)
  1 x 1832 Mushroom (G)
- 5mm (USH/8/UK6) crochet hook
- Tapestry needle

Tension

This is not essential for this pattern but each square motif is approximately 7 x 7in (18 x 18cm).

Note

You make two sides of nine squares. The squares are joined as you make them on the last round. Change the colours of your yarn up to round 5 but use yarn A for rounds 6–8.

Basic square

Round 1: Using 5mm hook and B, ch 4 sts, join with a sl st to form a ring.

Round 2: Ch 3 (this counts as the first tr), 11 tr into ring, sl st into 3rd ch at the beg of round (12 sts). Fasten off.

Round 3: Attach yarn C in any st, 3 ch (counts as 1 tr), 1 tr into same st, *2 tr next st; rep from * to end, join with a sl st into 3rd of 3 ch (24 sts). Fasten off.

Round 4: Attach yarn D in sp between any 2 tr groups, 3 ch (counts as the first tr), 2 tr into same sp, *3 tr between next 2 tr groups; rep from * to end, join with a sl st into 3rd of 3 ch (36 sts). Fasten off.

Round 5: Attach yarn E in sp between any 3 tr groups, 3 ch (counts as the first tr), 2 tr into same sp, 1 ch, *3 tr between next 3 tr group, 1 ch; rep from * to end, join with a sl st into 3rd of 3 ch. Fasten off.

Round 6: Attach yarn A in between any 3 tr groups, 3 ch (counts as the first tr), (2 tr, 3 ch, 3 tr) into sp, *1 ch (3 htr, 1 ch in sp between next two 3 tr groups) twice, (3 tr, 3 ch, 3 tr) between next two 3 tr groups; rep from * twice, 1 ch (3 htr, 1 ch in sp between next two 3 tr groups) twice, join with a sl st into 3rd of 3 ch.

Round 7: Sl st across to 3 ch corner sp, 3 ch (counts as the first tr), (2 tr, 3 ch, 3 tr) into sp, *1 ch (3 tr, 1 ch in next 1 ch sp) 3 times, (3 tr, 3 ch, 3 tr) between next 3 ch corner sp; rep from * twice, 1 ch, (3 tr, 1 ch in sp between next 1 ch sp) 3 times, join with a sl st into 3rd of 3 ch.

Round 8: Sl st across to 3 ch corner sp, 3 ch (counts as the first tr), (2 tr, 3 ch, 3 tr) into sp, *1 ch (3 tr, 1 ch in next 1 ch sp) 4 times, (3 tr, 3 ch, 3 tr) between next 3 ch corner sp; rep from * twice, 1 ch, (3 tr, 1 ch in sp between next 1 ch sp) 4 times, join with a sl st into 3rd of 3 ch.

Squares

2, 3, 4 and 7

Rounds 1–7: Work as for first square but change the colour combination using yarns.

Round 8: 3 ch (counts as the first tr), (2 tr, 3 ch, 3 tr) into sp, *1 ch (3 tr, 1 ch in next 1 ch sp) 4 times, 3 tr in 3 ch corner sp, 1 ch, 1 dc in 3 ch corner ch of previous square, 3 tr in same sp of the second square, (1 ch, dc into next 1 ch sp for previous square, 3 tr in next 1 ch sp of round 7 of the second square) 4 times, 1 ch, 3 tr in next 3 ch corner sp, 1 ch, 1 dc in 3 corner ch sp of first square, 3 tr in same sp of the second square, 1 ch, (3 tr, 1 ch in next 1 ch sp) 4 times, (3 tr, 3 ch, 3 tr) in next 3 ch corner sp, 1 ch, (3 tr, 1 ch in next 1 ch sp) 4 times, join with a sl st into 3rd of 3 ch. Fasten off.

Squares
5, 6, 8 and 9

Rounds 1–7: Work as for first square but change the colour combination using yarns.

Round 8: 3 ch (counts as the first tr), (2 tr, 3 ch, 3 tr) into sp, *1 ch (3 tr, 1 ch in next 1 ch sp) 4 times, *3 tr in 3 ch corner sp, 1 ch, 1 dc in 3 ch corner ch of previous square, 3 tr in same sp of the second square, (1 ch, dc into next 1 ch sp of previous square, 1 ch, 3 tr in next 1 ch sp of round 7 of the second square) 4 times; rep from *, 1 ch, 3 tr in next 3 ch corner sp, 1 ch, 1 dc in 3 corner ch sp of first square, 3 tr in same sp of the second square, 1 ch, (3 tr, 1 ch in next 1 ch sp) 4 times, join with a sl st into 3rd of 3 ch. Fasten off.

You should have two squares of nine joined crochet squares – three squares across and three down.

Neck opening
(back and front)

Work along the top of the square.

Row 1: With RS facing, join yarn A to right-hand 3 ch corner with a sl st, 3 ch (counts as first st), 1 tr in each st and ch to end, turn.

Rows 2–5: Ch 3, (counts as first st), 1 tr in each st to end, turn.

Shoulder join

For last side do not fasten off, with WS together, align both sides, sl st 20 sts, through both back loops. Fasten off.

Now work on second shoulder, turn work over so you are working on the second side.

Attach yarn A to right-hand edge with sl st, sl st 20 sts. Fasten off and weave in ends.

Sleeves

Open out the tank top, turn the work so that one long side seam is uppermost.

Row 1: With RS facing, at point X, join yarn A to right-hand 3 ch corner with a sl st, 3 ch (counts as first st), work evenly along the side to the tank top, 1 tr in each st and ch, work 2 tr in the side of tr sts until point Y, turn.

Row 2: Ch 3 (counts as first st), 1 tr in each st to end, turn.

Row 3: Ch 1 (counts as first st), 1 dc in each st to end, turn.

Side seams

With WS facing and yarn A, starting at the sleeve opening, sl st the sleeve and side seams together, until you are 2 tr clusters from the bottom of the top. Fasten off.

Repeat on the second side, but do not fasten off.

Bottom hem

Row 1: Turn work RS out, beginning at a side seam 1 ch, 1 dc in the top of each tr and ch, work (1 dc, 1 ch, 1 dc) in corner 3 ch sp, work along the bottom edge of first side, (1 dc, 1 ch, 1 dc) in corner 3 ch sp, then work 1 dc in top of tr and ch sp on small side slit. Rep for second side, turn.

Row 2: Ch 1 (counts as first st), 1 dc in each dc and (1 dc, 2 ch 1 dc) in corner ch sps to end. Fasten off.

Finishing

Weave in all ends.

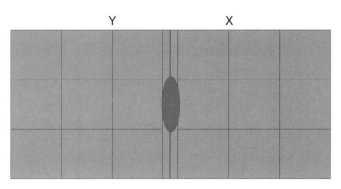

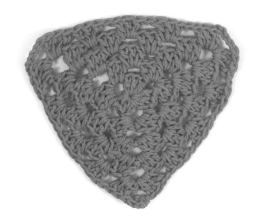

Triangle Bunting

If you are throwing a summer party or just feel like adding extra colour to your garden, then bunting is a fun little accessory that is quick to make. Change the colour scheme of your bunting to suit the occasion: soft pastels and cream to decorate a wedding, or traditional reds and greens to celebrate winter festivities. To ensure you have perfect pointed triangles, make sure you have enough time to block your bunting.

Finished size

To make a string of bunting 60in (1.5m) long with nine assorted triangles.

You will need

- Scheepjes Catona 4ply, 100% mercerized cotton (27yd/25m per 10g ball):
  1 x 106 Snow White (A)
  1 x 115 Hot Red, 281 Tangerine, 208 Yellow Gold, 205 Kiwi, 515 Emerald, 247 Bluebird, 226 Light Orchid, 519 Fresia and 240 Amethyst (B)
- 3.5mm (USE/4:UK9) crochet hook
- Tapestry needle

Tension

This is not essential but each triangle is approx 7 x 7 x 7in (17.75 x 17.75 x 17.75cm) using a 3.5mm hook.

Colour triangle
(make 9 in different colours)

Round 1: Using 3.5mm hook and B, ch 4 sts, join with a sl st to form a ring.

Round 2: Ch 8 (this counts as 1 tr, 5 ch), 3 tr, 5 ch, 3 tr, 6 ch, 2 tr, sl st into 3rd ch at the beg of round. (3 tr clusters). Do not fasten off.

Round 3: Sl st into corner ch sp, 8 ch, 3 tr into same sp, 1 ch, (3 tr, 5 ch, 3 tr) into next 5 ch sp, 1 ch, (3 tr, 6 ch 3 tr) in 6 ch sp, 1 ch, 2 tr in 5 ch sp, join with sl st into 3rd of 3 ch.

Round 4: Sl st into corner ch sp, 8 ch, 3 tr into same sp, 1 ch, 3 tr in next ch sp, 1 ch, (3 tr, 5 ch, 3 tr) into next 5 ch sp, 1 ch, 3 tr in next ch sp, 1 ch, (3 tr, 6 ch 3 tr) in 6 ch sp, 1 ch, 3 tr in next ch sp, 1 ch, 2 tr in 5 ch sp, join with sl st into 3rd of 3 ch.

Round 5: Sl st into corner ch sp, 8 ch, 3 tr into same sp, (1 ch, 3 tr in next ch sp) rep once, 1 ch, (3 tr, 5 ch, 3 tr) into next 5 ch sp, (1 ch, 3 tr in next ch sp) rep once, 1 ch, (3 tr, 6 ch 3 tr) in 6 ch sp, (1 ch, 3 tr in next ch sp) rep once, 1 ch, 2 tr in 5 ch sp, join with sl st into 3rd of 3 ch.

Round 6: Sl st into corner ch sp, 8 ch, 3 tr into same sp, (1 ch, 3 tr in next ch sp) rep twice, 1 ch, (3 tr, 5 ch, 3 tr) into next 5 ch sp, (1 ch, 3 tr in next ch sp) rep twice, 1 ch, (3 tr, 6 ch 3 tr) in 6 ch sp, (1 ch, 3 tr in next ch sp) rep twice, 1 ch, 2 tr in 5 ch sp, join with sl st into 3rd of 3 ch. Fasten off and weave in ends.

Finishing

Row 1: Using A and 3.5mm hook, ch 15, sl st in sixth ch from hook to create a loop, 1 dc in every st along the top edge of the triangle, *5 ch, dc in every st along top edge of next triangle; rep from * until all nine triangles have been attached, 15 ch, sl st in 10th ch from hook.
Fasten off and weave in ends.

Vibrant Tea Cosy

Crochet and tea are happy bedfellows. Nothing looks more welcoming and joyful than a pot of tea covered with a colourful tea cosy. There is no need to make a cosy any more complicated. Here the vibrant rainbow hues typify the vintage look, but it would also be great to make a version that matches your kitchen or tea set.

Finished size

6½in (16.5cm) wide and 8in (20cm) high with pompom, to fit a standard six-cup teapot

You will need

- Stylecraft Special DK, 100% acrylic (322yd/295m per 100g ball):
  1 x 1246 Lipstick (A)
  1 x 1711 Spice (B)
  1 x 1390 Clematis (C)
  1 x 1823 Mustard (D)
  1 x 1852 Apple (E)
  1 x 1003 Aster (F)
  1 x 1855 Proper Purple (G)
- 3.5mm (USE/4:UK9) crochet hook
- 3¼in (8cm) pompom maker
- Tapestry needle

Tension

This is not essential for this pattern but each square motif is approximately 7 x 7in (17 x 17cm).

Note

You will need to make two square motifs for this design. You will attach the two sides at the base to make space for the spout and the handle. The top of the cosy is gathered and then you place a pompom on top and secure with a few small stitches.

Basic square

(make 2)

Round 1: Using 3.5mm hook and A, ch 4 sts, join with a sl st to form a ring.

Round 2: Ch 6 (this counts as the first tr and 3 ch), (3 tr into ring, 3 ch) 3 times, 2 tr into ring, sl st into 3rd of 6 ch at the beg of round. Fasten off.

Round 3: Attach yarn B in any corner chain sp with a sl st, 6 ch (counts as the first tr and 3 ch), 3 tr into same ch sp, *1 ch, miss 3 tr, (3 tr, 3 ch, 3 tr) into next ch sp; rep from * twice, 1 ch, miss 3 tr, 2 tr into next ch sp, sl st into 3rd of 6 ch at beg of round. Fasten off.

Round 4: Attach yarn C in any corner chain sp with a sl st, 6 ch (counts as the first tr and 3 ch), 3 tr into same ch sp, *1 ch, miss 3 tr, 3 tr into next ch sp, 1 ch, miss 3 tr, (3 tr, 3 ch, 3 tr) into next ch sp; rep from * twice, 1 ch, miss 3 tr, 3 tr into next ch sp, 1 ch, miss 3 tr, 2 tr into next ch sp, sl st into 3rd of 6 ch at beg of round. Fasten off.

Round 5: Attach yarn D in any corner chain sp with a sl st, 6 ch (counts as the first tr and 3 ch), 3 tr into same ch sp, *(1 ch, miss 3 tr, 3 tr into next ch sp) twice, 1 ch, miss 3 tr, (3 tr, 3 ch, 3 tr) into next ch sp; rep from * twice, (1 ch, miss 3 tr, 3 tr into next ch sp) twice, 1 ch, miss 3 tr, 2 tr into next ch sp, sl st into 3rd of 6 ch at beg of round. Fasten off.

Round 6: Attach yarn E in any corner chain sp with a sl st, 6 ch (counts as the first tr and 3 ch), 3 tr into same ch sp, *(1 ch, miss 3 tr, 3 tr into next ch sp) 3 times, 1 ch, miss 3 tr, (3 tr, 3 ch, 3 tr) into next ch sp; rep from * twice, (1 ch, miss 3 tr, 3 tr into next ch sp) 3 times, 1 ch, miss 3 tr, 2 tr into next ch sp, sl st into 3rd of 6 ch at beg of round. Fasten off.

Round 7: Attach yarn F in any corner chain sp with a sl st, 6 ch (counts as the first tr and 3 ch), 3 tr into same ch sp, *(1 ch, miss 3 tr, 3 tr into next ch sp) 4 times, 1 ch, miss 3 tr, (3 tr, 3 ch, 3 tr) into next ch sp; rep from * twice, (1 ch, miss 3 tr, 3 tr into next ch sp) 4 times, 1 ch, miss 3 tr, 2 tr into next ch sp, sl st into 3rd of 6 ch at beg of round. Fasten off.

Round 8: Attach yarn G in any corner chain sp with a sl st, 6 ch (counts as the first tr and 3 ch), 3 tr into same ch sp, *(1 ch, miss 3 tr, 3 tr into next ch sp) 5 times, 1 ch, miss 3 tr, (3 tr, 3 ch, 3 tr) into next ch sp; rep from * twice, (1 ch, miss 3 tr, 3 tr into next ch sp) 5 times, 1 ch, miss 3 tr, 2 tr into next ch sp, sl st into 3rd of 6 ch at beg of round. Fasten off.

Round 9: Attach yarn A in any corner chain sp with a sl st, 6 ch (counts as the first tr and 3 ch), 3 tr into same ch sp, *(1 ch, miss 3 tr, 3 tr into next ch sp) 6 times, 1 ch, miss 3 tr, (3 tr, 3 ch, 3 tr) into next ch sp; rep from * twice, (1 ch, miss 3 tr, 3 tr into next ch sp) 6 times, 1 ch, miss 3 tr, 2 tr into next ch sp, sl st into 3rd of 6 ch at beg of round. Fasten off.

Finishing

Weave in ends and block each of your two squares. With wrong sides facing, using yarn A and a tapestry needle, sew the two bottom corners together. Using A, sew a running stitch along the top seams of the tea cosy and gather together. Sew the gather firmly. Make a pompom (see page 42) using A and sew securely to the top.

Fingerless Mittens

I find fingerless mittens so useful in the chilly seasons and almost always have a pair stashed in the pockets of every coat I own. I like this patten because the alternating colours of the treble stitches created a vibrant fairisle look to the cuffs.

Finished size

Mittens measure 4in (10cm) wide and 8in (20cm) long

You will need

- Stylecraft Special DK, 100% acrylic (322yd/295m per 100g ball):
  1 x 1823 Mustard (A)
  1 x 1843 Powder Pink (B)
  1 x 1711 Spice (C)
  1 x 1002 Black (D)
  1 x 1852 Apple (E)
  1 x 1005 Cream (F)
  1 x 1825 Lobelia (G)
- 3.5mm (UK9:USE/4) crochet hook
- Tapestry needle

Tension

Each square motif is approximately 4 x 4in (10 x 10cm). Tension is not essential for this pattern.

Note

You will need to make two square motifs for this design. You will then add on sections of crochet worked in rows to form the mittens.

Square
(make 2)

Round 1: Using 3.5mm hook and A, ch 4 sts, join with a sl st to form a ring.

Round 2: Ch 3 (this counts as the first tr), 11 tr into ring, sl st into 3rd ch at the beg of round (12 sts). Fasten off.

Round 3: Attach yarn B between any two treble sts, 3 ch (counts as 1 tr), 1 tr into same sp, *2 tr between next 2 sts; rep from * to end, join with a sl st into 3rd of 3 ch. Fasten off.

Round 4: Attach yarn C in sp between any 2 tr groups, 3 ch (counts as the first tr), 2 tr into same sp, *3 tr between next 2 tr groups; rep from * to end, join with a sl st into 3rd of 3 ch. Fasten off.

Round 5: Attach yarn D in between any 3 tr groups, 3 ch (counts as the first tr), (2 tr, 3 ch, 3 tr) into sp, *1 ch (3 htr, 1 ch in sp between next two 3 tr groups) twice, (3 tr, 3 ch, 3 tr) between next two 3 tr groups; rep from * twice, 1 ch (3 htr, 1 ch in sp between next two 3 tr groups) twice, join with a sl st into 3rd of 3 ch. Fasten off.

Round 6: Attach yarn E to corner chain sp, 1 ch, (1 dc, 1 ch, 2 dc) into sp, 1 dc into each st and 1 dc into every 1 ch, (2 dc, 1 ch, 2 dc) into every 3 ch sp, sl st into 1 ch at beg of round.

Round 7: Rep round 6 using yarn F.

Round 8: Rep round 6 using yarn D.

Fasten off and weave in ends.

Palm

Row 1: Using 3.5mm hook and D, attach yarn to any 1 ch on the corner of the square with a sl st, 1 ch, 1 dc in each dc and ch, turn (21 sts).

Row 2: 1 ch, 1 dc in each dc, turn (21 sts).

Rows 3–25: Work 23 rows straight. Fasten off.

Top

Fold your work in half so that the square is at the top and the palm is below. You will now work the top edging of the mitten in the round.

Row 1: Using 3.5mm hook and G, attach yarn to any 1 ch on the corner of the square with a sl st, 1 ch, work 40 dc evenly along square and side of the palm, join with sl st in 1 ch (40 sts). Fasten off.

Row 2: Attach yarn D to any dc, 2 ch, 1 htr in same st, *miss 1 dc, 1 ch, *htr2tog in next st; rep from * around, join with sl st to 2nd ch (20 htr clusters).

Row 3: Attach yarn F to any 1 ch sp, 2 ch, 1 htr in same st, *miss 1 htr2tog, 1 ch, *htr2tog in next ch sp; rep from * around, join with sl st to 2nd ch. (20 htr clusters). Fasten off.

Row 4: Rep row 3 using yarn D.

Row 5: 1 ch, 1 dc in each htr2tog and ch sp (40 sts).

Cuff

You will now work the cuff edging along the base of the mitten.

Row 1: Using 3.5mm hook and G, attach yarn to any st on the corner of the dc palm with a sl st, 1 ch, 1 dc in base of ch, 1 ch, miss 1 st, 1 dc in next st. Work 20 dc and 20 ch

evenly along square and side of the palm, join with sl st in 1 ch (40 sts). Fasten off.

Row 2: Attach yarn F to any ch sp, 3 ch, 1 tr in same st, *miss 1 dc, 1 ch, *tr2tog in next st; rep from * around, join with sl st to 2nd ch (20 tr clusters). Fasten off.

Row 3: Attach yarn G to any ch sp, 1 ch, 1 dc in base of ch, *1 ch, miss 1 st, 1 dc in next st; rep from * to end, sl st in 1 ch (40 sts). Fasten off.

Row 4: Rep row 3 using yarn E.

Row 5: Attach yarn D to any dc, 3 ch, 1 tr in same st, *miss 1 dc, 1 ch, *tr2tog in next st; rep from * around, join with sl st to 2nd ch (20 tr clusters).

Row 6: Attach yarn F to any 1 ch sp, 3 ch, 1 tr in same st, *miss 1 tr2tog, 1 ch, *tr2tog in next ch sp; rep from * around, join with sl st to 2nd ch (20 tr clusters). Fasten off.

Row 7: Rep row 6 using yarn D.

Finishing

Weave in all ends.

You will now attach the side seams together of each mitten allowing a hole in the seam for the thumb.

Left mitten

With RS together with the back of the granny square facing you, the top of the mitten should be to your right and the cuff should be on the left.

Using D, attach yarn with a slip stitch through both layers at the base of the dc row, 1 ch, 5 dc, now work just into the back palm material on the right side, work 12 sl sts, now work through both layers of the mitten, 12 dc. Fasten off and weave in ends.

Right mitten

With RS together with the back of the granny square facing you, the top of the mitten should be to your left and the cuff should be on the right.

Using D, attach yarn with a slip stitch through both layers at the base of the dc row, 1 ch, 12 dc, now work just into the back palm material on the right side, work 12 sl sts, now work through both layers of the mitten, 5 dc. Fasten off and weave in ends.

Boho Scarf

This is one of my favourite scarf patterns. You can create a colourful look and change the granny squares to match the colours of the season: brilliant and cosy in wool for the winter, a lighter and thinner version in cotton for milder seasons. I have put jaunty tassels at the ends but you could change these for fun pompoms.

Finished size

The scarf is approximately 6in (15cm) wide and 64in(163cm) long.

You will need

- Stylecraft Special DK, 100% acrylic (322yd/295m per 100g ball):
  1 x 1127 Peony (A)
  1 x 1843 Powder Pink (B)
  1 x 1080 Pale Rose (C)
  1 x 1083 Pomegranate (D)
  1 x 1123 Claret (E)
- 3.5mm (UK9:USE/4) crochet hook
- Tapestry needle

Tension

Each square motif is approximately 3½ x 3½in (9 x 9cm). Tension is not essential for this pattern.

Note

You will need to make 12 square and 2 triangle motifs for this design. The squares are joined together on the last row to create a long strip. You then add the triangle motifs at each end on their last row. You then work two rows of treble clusters around the edge of the joined motifs. Use a combination of any colours for your square and triangle motif but try to make sure the joining motifs are different to get that authentic vintage look.

First square

Round 1: Using 3.5mm hook and A, ch 4 sts, join with a sl st to form a ring.

Round 2: Ch 3 (this counts as the first tr), 11 tr into ring, sl st into 3rd ch at the beg of round (12 sts). Fasten off.

Round 3: Attach yarn C in any st, 3 ch (counts as 1 tr), 1 tr into same st, *2 tr next st; rep from * to end, join with a sl st into 3rd of 3 ch. Fasten off.

Round 4: Attach yarn B in sp between any 2 tr groups, 3 ch (counts as the first tr), 2 tr into same sp, *3 tr between next 2 tr groups; rep from * to end, join with a sl st into 3rd of 3 ch. Fasten off.

Round 5: Attach yarn D in between any 3 tr groups, 3 ch (counts as the first tr), (2 tr, 3 ch, 3 tr) into sp, *1 ch (3 htr, 1 ch, in sp between next two 3 tr groups) twice, (3 tr, 3 ch, 3 tr) between next two 3 tr groups; rep from * twice, 1 ch (3 htr, 1 ch, in sp between next two 3 tr groups) twice, join with a sl st into 3rd of 3 ch. Fasten off.

Round 6: Attach yarn E in any 3 ch corner sp, 3 ch (counts as the first tr), (2 tr, 3 ch, 3 tr) into sp, *1 ch (3 tr, 1 ch, in next 1 ch sp) 3 times, (3 tr, 3 ch, 3 tr) in next 3 ch corner sp; rep from * twice, 1 ch, (3 tr, 1 ch, in next 1 ch sp) 3 times, join with a sl st into 3rd of 3 ch. Fasten off.

Following 2–12 squares

Rounds 1–5: Work as for first square but change the colour combination using yarns.

Round 6: Attach yarn in any 3 ch corner sp, 3 ch (counts as the first tr), (2 tr, 3 ch, 3 tr) into sp, *1 ch (3 tr, 1 ch, in next 1 ch sp) 3 times, 3 tr in 3 ch corner sp, 1 ch, 1 dc in 3 ch corner sp of previous square, 3 tr in same sp of the second square, (1 ch, dc into next 1 ch sp for previous square, 3 tr in next 1 ch sp of the second square) 3 times,1 ch, 3 tr in next 3 ch corner sp, 1 ch, 1 dc in 3 corner ch sp of first square, 3 tr in same sp of the second square, 1 ch, (3 tr, 1 ch in sp) 3 times, (3 tr, 3 ch, 3 tr) in next 3 ch corner sp, 1 ch, (3 tr, 1 ch, in next 1 ch sp) 3 times, join with a sl st into 3rd of 3 ch. Fasten off.

Triangle
(make 2)

Round 1: Using 3.5mm hook and A, ch 4 sts, join with a sl st to form a ring.

Round 2: Ch 3 (this counts as the first tr), 8 tr into ring, sl st into 3rd ch at the beg of round (9 sts). Fasten off.

Round 3: Attach yarn D in any st, 3 ch (counts as 1 tr), 1 tr into same st, *2 tr in next st; rep from * to end, join with a sl st into 3rd of 3 ch. Fasten off.

Round 4: Attach yarn C in sp between any 2 tr groups, 3 ch (counts as the first tr), 2 tr into same sp, *3 tr between next 2 tr groups, 2 ch; rep from * to end, join with a sl st into 3rd of 3 ch. Fasten off.

Round 5: Attach yarn D in between any 3 tr groups, 3 ch (counts as the first tr), (2 tr, 3 ch, 3 tr) into sp, *1 ch (3 htr, 1 ch, in sp between next two 3 tr groups) twice, (3 tr, 3 ch, 3 tr) between next two 3 tr groups; rep from *, 1 ch (3 htr, 1 ch, in sp between next two 3 tr groups) twice, join with a sl st into 3rd of 3 ch. Fasten off.

You will now attach your triangles to the end of the long strip of granny squares.

Round 6: Attach yarn B in any 3 ch corner sp, 3 ch (counts as the first tr), (2 tr, 3 ch, 3 tr) into sp, *1 ch (3 tr, 1 ch, in next 1 ch sp) 3 times, 3 tr in 3 ch corner sp, 1 ch, 1 dc in 3 ch corner ch of the square, 3 tr in same sp of the triangle, (1 ch, dc into next 1 ch sp for the square, 3 tr in next 1 ch sp of the triangle) 3 times, 1 ch, 3 tr in next 3 ch corner sp, 1 ch, 1 dc in 3 corner ch sp of first square, 3 tr in same sp of the triangle, 1 ch, (3 tr, 1 ch, in next sp) three times, join with a sl st into 3rd of 3 ch. Fasten off.

Edging

Round 1: Using 3.5mm hook and D, attach yarn to a triangle corner sp at one end of the scarf, 3 ch (counts as the first tr), (2 tr, 3 ch, 3 tr) into sp, *(1 ch, 3 tr in next 1 ch sp) 4 times, 1 ch, 3 tr in sp between next 2 motifs; rep from * around the edge of the scarf, working (3 tr, 3 ch, 3 tr) in the point of the second triangle, (1 ch, 3 tr in next 1 ch sp) around, 1 ch, join with a sl st into 3rd of 3 ch. Fasten off.

Round 2: Join yarn A to a 3 ch corner sp at the end of the scarf, 3 ch (counts as the first tr) (2 tr, 3 ch, 3 tr) into sp, (1 ch, 3 tr in next 1 ch sp) around, working (3 tr, 3 ch, 3 tr) in the point of the second triangle, (1 ch, 3 tr in next 1 ch sp) around, 1 ch join with a sl st into 3rd of 3 ch.

Tassels
(make 2)

To make the tassels, fold a 4 x 4in (10 x 10cm) piece of card in half. Place a 6in (15cm) strand of yarn along the folded edge and then wrap the folded card 30 times. Knot the strand of yarn firmly on the top of the wrap. Cut the wrap of wool at the other end. Slip the card out. Then about ½in (1cm) from the top of the tassel, wind another strand of wool round to enclose the wool and create the tassel. Sew firmly to the end of the scarf.

Chain-link Garland

Creating colourful and vibrant accessories for parties and celebrations is one of my favourite things to do. Crochet is so adaptable and if you make your decorations in cotton yarns they will last well and look festive throughout the summer.

Finished size

Each chain link is 8½in (22cm) wide and 1½in (4cm) deep. A set of 12 linked chains is approximately 41in (104cm) long.

You will need

- Scheepjes Catona 4ply, 100% mercerized cotton (27yd/25m per 10g ball):
  1 x 281 Tangerine (A)
  1 x 515 Emerald (B)
  I have used a variety of colours to create the look of the garland. Choose vibrant tones from your stash.
- 3.5mm (USE/4:UK9) crochet hook

Tension

Tension is not essential for this project.

Note

If using up yarn remnants, make sure the weight of the yarn is the same throughout the project.

Chain loops

Round 1: Using 3.5mm hook and yarn A, ch 34 sts, 3 tr in 6th ch from hook, miss 2 ch, *3 tr in next ch, miss 2 ch; rep from * 7 times more, 1 tr in last ch. Fasten off yarn A.
You will now work around the treble strip on 4 sides.

Round 2: Using yarn B, join yarn to starting ch space of round 1, 5 ch (counts as 1 tr and 2 ch), 3 tr in same ch sp, 1 ch, *(3 tr, 1 ch) in next ch sp; rep from * 7 times more, (3 tr, 2 ch, 3 tr, 2 ch, 3 tr) in sp created by last tr of previous round (two corners made), now work on the bottom edge of the foundation ch, 1 ch, (3 tr, 1 ch) 8 times, 3 tr, 2 ch, 2 tr in 5 ch sp, sl st into 3rd ch at the beg of round. Leave a 4in (10cm) tail of yarn.

Finishing

Sew short ends of the crochet together to form a loop. Make 11 further strips and loop through a previously made loop before sewing the ends together. Weave in all ends.

Granny Square Hat

I love crocheting hats. In wool they are fabulously cosy for winter and yet in summer made in cotton they provide a wonderful festival cover-up to keep the sun off your head.

Finished size

The hat is approximately 8in (20cm) deep.

You will need

- Stylecraft Special DK, 100% acrylic (322yd/295m) per 100g ball):
  1 x 1127 Peony (A)
  1 x 1843 Powder Pink (B)
  1 x 1080 Pale Rose (C)
  1 x 1083 Pomegranate (D)
  1 x 1123 Claret (E)
- 3.5mm (UK9:USE/4) crochet hook
- Tapestry needle

Tension

Each square motif is approximately 3½ x 3½in (9 x 9cm). Tension is not essential for this pattern.

Note

You will need to make six square motifs for this design. The squares are joined together on the last row. You then add the crochet for the crown to one long edge and then work the stitches for the brim on the other long edge. The last round on the squares and the rest of the hat is worked in yarn A.

First square

Round 1: Using 3.5mm hook and B, ch 4 sts, join with a sl st to form a ring.

Round 2: Ch 3 (this counts as the first tr), 11 tr into ring, sl st into 3rd ch at the beg of round (12 sts). Fasten off.

Round 3: Attach yarn D between any 2 tr sts, 3 ch (counts as 1 tr), 1 tr into same sp, *2 tr between next 2 sts; rep from * to end, join with a sl st into 3rd of 3 ch. Fasten off.

Round 4: Attach yarn C in sp between any 2 tr groups, 3 ch (counts as the first tr), 2 tr into same sp, *3 tr between next 2 tr groups; rep from * to end, join with a sl st into 3rd of 3 ch. Fasten off.

Round 5: Attach yarn A in between any 3 tr groups, 3 ch (counts as the first tr), (2 tr, 3 ch, 3 tr) into sp, *1 ch (3 htr, 1 ch in sp between next two 3 tr groups) twice, (3 tr, 3 ch, 3 tr) between next two 3 tr groups; rep from * twice, 1 ch (3 htr, 1 ch in sp between next two 3 tr groups) twice, join with a sl st into 3rd of 3 ch. Fasten off.

Following 2–5 squares

Rounds 1–4: Work as for first square but change the colour combination using yarns B, C, D and E.

Round 5: Attach yarn A in between any 3 tr groups, 3 ch (counts as the first tr), (2 tr, 3 ch, 3 tr) into sp, *1 ch (3 htr, 1 ch in sp between next two 3 tr groups) twice, 3 tr between next two 3 tr groups, 1 ch, 1 dc in 3 ch corner ch of first square, 3 tr in same sp of the second square, (1 ch, dc into next 1 ch sp for first square, 3 htr in next 1 ch sp of round 4 of the second square) twice, 1 ch, 3 htr between next two tr groups, 1 ch, 1 dc in 3 corner ch sp of first square, 3 tr in same sp of the second square, 1 ch (3 htr, 1 ch in sp between next two 3 tr groups) twice, (3 tr, 3 ch, 3 tr) between next two 3 tr groups, 1 ch (3 htr, 1 ch in sp between next two 3 tr groups) twice; join with a sl st into 3rd of 3 ch. Fasten off.

Following sixth square

Rounds 1–4: Work as for first square but change the colour combination using yarns B, C, D and E.

Round 5: Using yarn A, join your square to both the first granny square and the fifth granny square in the join as you go method (see page 133). This will create a circular loop.

Crown

Using 3.5mm hook and A, place one edge of the loop of granny squares uppermost, attach yarn to any corner sp between two granny squares. You will now work in rounds.

Round 1: 3 ch (counts as the first tr),

2 tr into same sp, miss 3 ch corner sp and 3 tr, *(1 ch, 3 tr in next 1 ch sp) 3 times, 3 tr in sp between next 2 squares; rep from * 4 times, (1 ch, 3 tr in next 1 ch sp) 3 times, 1 ch, join with a sl st into 3rd of 3 ch (24 tr clusters).

Rounds 2–5: Sl st across the top of 3 tr and into 1 ch sp, 3 ch (counts as the first tr), 2 tr into same sp, (1 ch, 3 tr in next 1 ch sp) around, 1 ch join with a sl st into 3rd of 3 ch.

Round 6: Sl st across the top of 3 tr and into 1 ch sp, 3 ch (counts as the first tr), 2 tr into same sp, (1 ch, 3 tr in next 1 ch sp), 1 ch, *htr2tog in next 2 spaces, (1 ch, 3 tr in next 1 ch sp) twice; rep from * 3 times, htr2tog in next 2 spaces, 1 ch, join with a sl st into 3rd of 3 ch (18 tr clusters).

Round 7: Sl st across the top of 3 tr and into 1 ch sp, 3 ch (counts as the first tr), 2 tr into same sp, 1 ch, *htr2tog in next 2 spaces, 1 ch, 3 tr in next 1 ch sp, 1 ch; rep from * 3 times, htr2tog in next 2 spaces, 1 ch, join with a sl st into 3rd of 3 ch (12 tr clusters).

Round 8: Sl st across the top of 3 tr and into 1 ch sp, 3 ch (counts as the first tr), 1 tr, leave both loops on hook and htr2tog in next space and yo and pull through all 4 loops, *htr2tog in next 2 spaces, 4 times; rep from *, join with a sl st into 3rd of 3 ch (6 tr clusters).

Fasten off and leave a long tail of yarn. Using a tapestry needle, sew small stitches along the top of the tr clusters and gather together. Fasten off securely and weave in ends.

Brim

Turn your work around to ensure that the other side of the granny square loop is uppermost.

You will now work the brim edging along the base of the granny squares.

Round 1: Using 3.5mm hook and A, attach yarn to any st on the corner ch of a granny square with a sl st, 1 ch, 1 dc in each dc and ch evenly along the base of the hat. Do not fasten off but work in a spiral (102 sts).

Rows 2–5: 1 ch, 1 dc tbl in each dc (102 sts).

Fasten off and weave in ends.

Hexagon Pot Holder

There is no higher compliment that I can give an object than it is a 'boon'. The definition in my mind is an object which really is marvellous. I don't think I would ever do without a potholder now in the kitchen. They are so handy for lifting hot pans and specifically saucepan lids. Less cumbersome than oven gloves, potholders can also be very attractive and you can make them in all your favourite colours.

Finished size

7in (18cm) wide

You will need

- Stylecraft Bellissima DK,
  100% acrylic (293yd/268m
  per 100g ball):
  1 x 3978 Flaming Fuchsia (A)
  1 x 3921 Single Cream (B)
  1 x 7216 Luscious Leaf (C)
  1 x 3932 Rio Red (F)
- Stylecraft Bambino DK,
  100% acrylic (293yd/268m
  per 100g ball):
  1 x 7118 Little Boy Blue (D)
  1 x 7113 Soft Pink (E)
- 3.5mm (US4/E:UK9) crochet hook
- A square of felt, 7x 7in (18 x 18cm)
- Tapestry needle

Tension

This is not essential for this pattern.

Note

You will need to make two hexagon
motifs for this design. You then
slip stitch the two sides and base
together and then chain stitch a
handy loop for it to hang next to
your stove.

Hexagon

(make 2)

Round 1: Using 3.5mm hook and
A, ch 4 sts, join with a sl st to form
a ring.

Round 2: Ch 4 (this counts as the
first tr and 1 ch), (3 tr into ring, 1 ch)
5 times, 2 tr into ring, sl st into 3rd of
6 ch at the beg of round. Fasten off.

Round 3: Attach yarn B in any chain
sp with a sl st, 5 ch (counts as the first
tr and 2 ch), 2 tr into same ch sp,
*1 ch, miss 3 tr, (2 tr, 2 ch, 2 tr) into
next ch sp; rep from * 4 times, 1 ch,
miss 3 tr, 1 tr into next ch sp, sl st into
3rd of 5 ch at beg of round.
Fasten off.

Round 4: Attach yarn C in any corner
2 chain sp with a sl st, 5 ch (counts as
the first tr and 2 ch), 2 tr into same ch
sp, *1 ch, miss 2 tr, 2 tr into next ch
sp, 1 ch, miss 2 tr, (2 tr, 2 ch, 2 tr)
into next ch sp; rep from * 4 times,
1 ch, miss 2 tr, 2 tr into next ch sp,
1 ch, miss 2 tr, 1 tr into next ch sp, sl
st into 3rd of 5 ch at beg of round.
Fasten off.

Round 5: Attach yarn D in any corner
2 chain sp with a sl st, 5 ch (counts as
the first tr and 2 ch), 2 tr into same ch
sp, *(1 ch, miss 2 tr, 2 tr into next ch
sp) twice, 1 ch, miss 2 tr, (2 tr, 2 ch,
2 tr) into next ch sp; rep from * 4
times, (1 ch, miss 2 tr, 2 tr into next
ch sp) twice, 1 ch, miss 1 tr, 1 tr into
next ch sp, sl st into 3rd of 5 ch at
beg of round. Fasten off.

Round 6: Attach yarn E in any corner
2 chain sp with a sl st, 5 ch (counts
as the first tr and 2 ch), 2 tr into same
ch sp, *(1 ch, miss 2 tr, 2 tr into next
ch sp) 3 times, 1 ch, miss 2 tr, (2 tr,
2 ch, 2 tr) into next ch sp; rep from *
4 times, (1 ch, miss 2 tr, 2 tr into next
ch sp) 3 times, 1 ch, miss 2 tr, 1 tr into
next ch sp, sl st into 3rd of 5 ch at
beg of round. Fasten off.

Round 7: Attach yarn F in any corner
chain sp with a sl st, 5 ch (counts as
the first tr and 2 ch), 2 tr into same
ch sp, *(1 ch, miss 2 tr, 2 tr into next
ch sp) 4 times, 1 ch, miss 2 tr, (2 tr,
2 ch, 2 tr) into next ch sp; rep from *
4 times, (1 ch, miss 2 tr, 2 tr into next
ch sp) 4 times, 1 ch, miss 2 tr, 1 tr into
next ch sp, sl st into 3rd of 5 ch at
beg of round. Fasten off.

Finishing

Weave in ends and block each of
your hexagons. Using the crocheted
hexagon as a guide, cut a piece
of felt slightly smaller than the
crocheted motif. With wrong sides
facing, and the felt between the two
pieces of crochet, working through
both layers join yarn A two stitches
after any corner, 1 ch, 1 dc in every
tr and ch sp, 2 dc in every corner,
around, finish 2 sts before last
corner, 6 ch, miss next 2 sts, corner
and sl st at base of beg ch, turn, work
8 dc into ch loop, sl st at base of 6 ch
loop. Fasten off and weave in ends.

Beach Bag

This fun-looking bag has all the joyful appeal of boho chic.
Surprisingly spacious, it is ideal to store your towel
and costume on a trip to the beach.

Finished size

14in (36cm) wide and 14in (36cm) long, including handles

You will need

- Stylecraft Naturals Organic DK, 100% cotton (115yd/105m per 50g ball):
  1 x 7179 Flamingo (A)
  1 x 7170 Poppy (B)
  1 x 7181 Carrot (C)
  1 x 7175 Citronelle (D)
  1 x 7191 Jade (E)
  1 x 7198 Azure (F)
  1 x 7185 Amethyst (G)
- 4mm (UK8:USG/6) crochet hook
- Tapestry needle

Tension

This is not essential but each square is approximately 6 x 6in (15 x 15cm) using a 4mm hook.

Basic square

Round 1: Using 4mm hook and A, ch 4 sts, join with a sl st to form a ring.

Round 2: Ch 3 (this counts as the first tr), 11 tr into ring, sl st into 3rd ch at the beg of round (12 sts).
Fasten off.

Round 3: Attach yarn B between any two treble sts, 3 ch (counts as 1 tr), 1 tr into same sp, *2 tr between next 2 sts; rep from * to end, join with a sl st into 3rd of 3 ch. Fasten off.

Round 4: Attach yarn C in sp between any 2 tr groups, 3 ch (counts as the first tr), 2 tr into same sp, *3 tr between next 2 tr groups; rep from * to end, join with a sl st into 3rd of 3 ch. Fasten off.

Round 5: Attach yarn D in between any 3 tr groups, 3 ch (counts as the first tr), (2 tr, 3 ch, 3 tr) into sp, *1 ch (3 htr, 1 ch in sp between next two 3 tr groups) twice, (3 tr, 3 ch, 3 tr) between next two 3 tr groups; rep from * twice, 1 ch (3 htr, 1 ch in sp between next two 3 tr groups) twice, join with a sl st into 3rd of 3 ch.

Round 6: Change to E, attach yarn to any 3 ch sp, (3 ch, 2 tr, 3 ch, 3 tr, 1 ch) in ch sp, (3 tr, 1 ch) in next 3 ch sps, *(3 tr, 3 ch, 3 tr, 1 ch) in next 3 ch sp, (3 tr, 1 ch) in next 3 ch sps; rep from * twice more, sl st in 3 ch (20 tr clusters).

Round 7: Change to F, attach yarn to any 3 ch sp, (3 ch, 2 tr, 3 ch, 3 tr, 1 ch) in ch sp, (3 tr, 1 ch) in next 4 ch sps, *(3 tr, 3 ch, 3 tr, 1 ch) in next 3 ch sp, (3 tr, 1 ch) in next 4 ch sps; rep from * twice more, sl st in 3 ch (24 tr clusters).
Fasten off and weave in ends.

Round 8: Sl st across to corner chain sp, 1 ch, (2 dc, 1 ch, 2 dc) into sp, 1 dc into each st and 1 dc into every 1 ch, (2 dc, 1 ch, 2 dc) into every 3 ch sp, sl st into 1 ch at beg of round (108 sts).

Complete eight squares using a combination of different colours.

Joining the squares

Weave in ends and block each of your squares. Using the diagram on page 100 as a guide, join the squares together using yarn A, by placing a sl st in the back loop of each st in each square.

In the diagram you join the edges of the squares together so that points meet where the letter is the same; sew the edges together where colours match.

Top side edging

Round 1: Using 4mm hook and E, attach yarn to a top corner of a square at the edge of the bag with a sl st: this is shown as * on the diagram. (3 ch, 2 tr, 3 ch, 3 tr, 1 ch) in ch sp, miss 3 sts, 3 tr in next ch sp,

1 ch, *(miss 3 sts, 3 tr, 1 ch) 4 times, miss 5 sts, 1 dtr in corner of base square, miss 5 sts, 3 tr in next ch sp, 1 ch, (miss 3 sts, 3 tr, 1 ch) 4 times, miss 3 sts, (3 tr, 3 ch, 3 tr, 1 ch) in corner ch sp; rep from * around, sl st into top of 3 ch. Fasten off.

Round 2: Join next colour into corner ch sp, (3 ch, 2 tr, 3 ch, 3 tr, 1 ch) in ch sp, *(miss 3 tr group, 3 tr in ch sp, 1 ch) 5 times, miss 3 tr group, 1 dtr in dtr, (miss 3 tr group, 3 tr in ch sp, 1 ch) 5 times, miss 3 tr group, (3 tr, 3 ch, 3 tr, 1 ch) in corner ch sp, rep from * around, sl st into top of 3 ch.
Rep round 2, 3 more times, using different colours.

Round 6: Attach yarn to top 3 ch sp, 1 ch, *(1 dc, 1 ch, 1 dc) in ch sp, 22 dc, dc3tog (working over last st, dtr, and next st), 22 dc; rep from * 3 times, do not fasten off but work in continuous spirals until 5 rounds have been completed. Fasten off and weave in ends.

Bag handle
(make 2)

The handles are worked with RS facing at all times. Do not turn the work but start each new row to the right of the crochet and work through the back loop only.

Row 1: With RS facing and using 4mm hook and A, ch 41 sts.

Do not turn.
Rows 2–6: Change yarn, 1 ch, 1 dc tbl at base of ch, 1 dc tbl to end. Fasten off (40 sts).
Row 7: Change to yarn A, sl st in each st to end. Fasten off and weave in ends.

You can create extra strength to your handles by sewing spare ribbon to the underside of the handles.

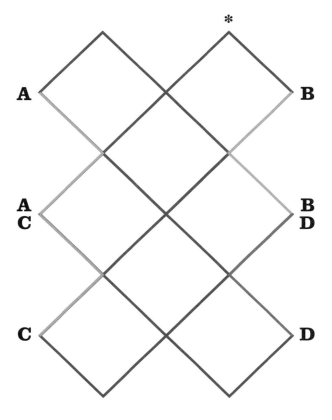

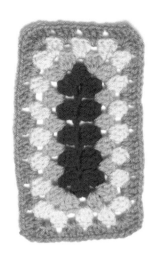

Rectangle Tote Bag

Having a colourful tote bag is perfect for work or shopping and it's great to have one that is sizeable enough to hold everything you will need to carry. I have lined mine with felt for extra sturdiness. These colours are the ultimate vintage combination.

Finished size

17in (43cm) wide and 20in (50cm) deep

You will need

- Stylecraft Special Aran, 100% acrylic (214yd/196m per 100g ball):
  1 x 1246 Lipstick (A)
  1 x 1241 Fondant (B)
  1 x 1005 Cream (C)
  1 x 1019 Cloud Blue (D)
  1 x 1852 Apple (E)
  1 x 1826 Kelly Green (F)
  1 x 1218 Parchment (G)
- 4mm (USG/6:UK8) crochet hook
- Tapestry needle and 20 x 20 in (50 x 50cm) of felt if you would like to line your tote bag.

Tension

Tension is not essential for this project.

Note

The rectangle is created by work around two sides of the starting chain.

Sides
(make 2)

Round 1: Using 4mm hook and yarn A, ch 16 sts, 3 tr in 7th ch from hook, (miss 2 ch, 3 tr in next ch, 1 ch) twice, (3 tr, 3 ch, 3 tr, 3 ch, 3 tr) in last ch st, (two corners made), (miss 2 ch, 3 tr in next ch, 1 ch) twice, (3 tr, 3 ch, 2 tr) in first ch st, join with a sl st into 3rd of 3 ch (10 tr clusters). Fasten off.

Round 2: Attach B in any corner chain sp with a sl st, 6 ch (counts as the first tr and 3 ch), 3 tr into same ch sp, (1 ch, miss 3 tr, 3 tr into next ch sp) 3 times, 1 ch, miss 3 tr, (3 tr, 3 ch, 3 tr) into next ch sp, 1 ch, (3 tr, 3 ch, 3 tr) into next ch sp, (1 ch, miss 3 tr, 3 tr into next ch sp) 3 times, 1 ch, miss 3 tr, (3 tr, 3 ch, 3 tr) into next ch sp, 1 ch, 2 tr into next ch sp, sl st into 3rd of 6 ch at beg of round. Fasten off.

Round 3: Attach C in any corner chain sp with a sl st, 6 ch (counts as the first tr and 3 ch), 3 tr into same ch sp, (1 ch, 3 tr into next ch sp) 4 times, 1 ch, (3 tr, 3 ch, 3 tr) into next ch sp, 1 ch, 3 tr in next ch sp, 1 ch, (3 tr, 3 ch, 3 tr) into next ch sp, (1 ch, 3 tr into next ch sp) 4 times, 1 ch, (3 tr, 3 ch, 3 tr) into next ch sp, 1 ch, 3 tr in next ch sp, 1 ch, 2 tr into next ch sp, sl st into 3rd of 6 ch at beg of round. Fasten off.

Round 4: Attach D in any corner chain sp with a sl st, 6 ch (counts as the first tr and 3 ch), 3 tr into same ch sp, (1 ch, 3 tr into next ch sp) 5 times, 1 ch, (3 tr, 3 ch, 3 tr) into next ch sp, (1 ch, 3 tr in next ch sp) twice, 1 ch, (3 tr, 3 ch, 3 tr) into next ch sp, (1 ch, 3 tr into next ch sp) 5 times, 1 ch, (3 tr, 3 ch, 3 tr) into next ch sp, (1 ch, 3 tr in next ch sp) twice, 1 ch, 2 tr into next ch sp, sl st into 3rd of 6 ch at beg of round. Fasten off.

Continue increasing the granny square in this manner using the colour sequence:
E, F, G, A, B, C, D, E, F, G

Work until you have 62 treble clusters ending with a row in G. You will now work in rows along three sides of the rectangle.

Row 1: With RS facing and the long edge uppermost, attach yarn G to the top right-hand corner ch sp with a sl st, 1 dc into same ch sp, 1 dc into each tr and 1 dc into every 1 ch, (1 dc, 1 ch, 1 dc) into every 3 ch sp, along three sides. End with the 4th 3 ch corner sp, turn. Do not fasten off.

Rows 2–8: 1 ch, 1 dc at base of ch, 1 dc into each st and ch sp, turn.

Rows 9–10: Change to yarn C, 1 ch, 1 dc at base of ch, 1 dc into each st, turn.

Rows 11–12: Change to yarn B, 1 ch, 1 dc at base of ch, 1 dc into each st, turn.

Row 13: Change to yarn A, 1 ch, 1 dc at base of ch, 1 dc into each st, turn.

Rectangle Tote Bag

When you have completed the last rectangle, do not fasten off. With WS facing, align the two rectangles and join them by working in yarn A through the back loop or both row 13 with a slip stitch.

Top side edging

Round 1: Using 4mm hook and G, attach yarn to a top corner of a square at the edge of the bag with a sl st, 1 ch, 1 dc in st at base of ch, work 1 dc in each tr and ch sp along the top of bag sides, work in continuous spirals until 7 rounds have been completed. Fasten off and weave in ends.

Bag handles
(make 2)

Row 1: Using 4mm hook and G, ch 91 sts, 1 dc in second ch from hook, 1 dc to end, turn. (90 sts).
Rows 2–7: Ch 1, 1 dc to end, turn. (90 sts).
Fasten off and weave in ends.

You can create extra strength to your handles by sewing spare felt or ribbon to the underside of the handles. Sew the bag handles 2in (5cm) from the side edges of the bag.

Colour Block Cushion

I love a checked fabric and just by using simple squares you can create a wonderful vibrant pattern. For this cushion I have chosen jewel-like colours that have a rich tonal effect.

Finished size

To fit an 18 x 18in (46 x 46cm) cushion pad

You will need

- Stylecraft Bellissima DK, 100% acrylic (293yd/268m per 100g ball):
  1 x 3932 Rio Red (A)
  1 x 3977 Papaya Punch (B)
  1 x 3978 Flaming Fuchsia (C)
  1 x 3926 Sugar Snap (D)
  1 x 3927 Overly Olive (E)
  1 x 7219 Denim Dungarees (F)
  1 x 7217 Orchid Haze (G)
- Stylecraft Bambino DK, 100% acrylic (293yd/268m per 100g ball):
  1 x 7113 Soft Pink (H)
- 3.5mm (US4/E:UK9) crochet hook
- Tapestry needle

Tension

Each square is approximately 2 x 2in (5 x 5cm) using a 3.5mm hook.

Basic square

Using 3.5mm hook A, ch 4 sts, join with a sl st to form a ring.

Round 1: Ch 5 (this counts as 1 tr, 2 ch), 3 tr into ring, *3 ch, 3 tr; rep from * twice, 3 ch, 2 tr, sl st into 3rd ch at the beg of round (4 tr clusters). Do not fasten off.

Round 2: Sl st into 3 ch sp, 3 ch (counts as 1 tr), (1 tr, 2 ch, 2 tr) into same ch sp, *1 tr into each tr across side of square, (2 tr, 2 ch, 2 tr) into next 3 ch sp; rep from * twice, 1 tr in each tr across side of square, join with a sl st into 3rd of 3 ch.

Make 64 squares: Make 8 squares in each colour and join together strips of alternate squares of A&B, C&H, D&E, F&G. Weave in all ends. Block each square gently so that the edges are straight and the corners are sharper.

Using the photo as a guide, sew the squares together. With RS together, whip stitch (see page 38) the outer loops of each square together. Attach the tonal colours together first to create strips of 8 squares and then work across the strips of 8 squares.

I have sewn the cushion cover to the front of a covered cushion pad, but alternatively you have enough yarn to make a second side and join both squares together.

Chunky First Blanket

Crocheting for a newborn is very special. Frequently it is the excitement of a new arrival that inspires people to learn to crochet. This simple pattern is ideal for such an occasion. The pattern grows quickly and the colours you choose for the design can match with colours chosen for a nursery or pram.

Finished size

Blanket measures 32 x 32in
(81 x 81cm)

You will need

- James C Brett Chunky with Merino,
  20% polyamide, 10% Wool,
  70% acrylic (164yd/150m per
  100g ball):
  2 x CM01 White (A)
  2 x CM21 Light Grey (B)
  1 x CM25 Dusky Pink (C)
  1 x CM27 Lilac (D)
- 6mm (USJ/10:UK4) crochet hook
- Tapestry needle

Tension

This is not essential for this pattern.

Blanket

Round 1: Using 6mm hook and C, ch
4 sts, join with a sl st to form a ring.
Round 2: Ch 3 (this counts as the first
tr), 2 tr into ring, 2 ch, *3 tr into ring,
2 ch; rep from * twice, join with sl st
into 3rd of 3 ch. Break off yarn C.
Round 3: Attach yarn A in any 2 ch
sp with a sl st, 1 ch, (1 dc, 3 ch, 1 dc)
into same sp, 3 ch, * (1 dc, 3 ch, 1 dc)
into next 2 ch sp, 3 ch; rep from *
twice, join with sl st to first dc. (Four
corners made.) Break off yarn A.
Round 4: Attach yarn B in any 3 ch
corner sp with a sl st, 3 ch (counts as
the first tr), (2 tr, 3 ch,3 tr) into same
ch sp, *1 ch, 3 tr into next 3 ch sp,
1 ch, *(3 tr, 3 ch, 3 tr) into next ch sp,
1 ch, 3 tr into next 3 ch sp, 1 ch; rep
from * twice, join with sl st into 3rd of
3 ch at beg of round. Break off yarn B.
Round 5: Attach yarn A in any corner
3 ch sp with a sl st, 1 ch (1 dc, 3 ch,
1 dc) into same sp, 3 ch, (1 dc into
next 1 ch sp, 3 ch) twice, * (1 dc,
3 ch, 1 dc) into next 3 ch corner sp,
3 ch, (1 dc into next 1 ch sp, 3 ch)
twice; rep from * twice, join with sl st
into first dc. Break off yarn A.
Round 6: Attach yarn D to any 3 ch
corner sp, 3 ch (counts as 1 tr), (2 tr,
3 ch, 3 tr) into same sp, 1 ch, (3 tr into
next 3 ch sp, 1 ch) 3 times, * (3 tr,
3 ch, 3 tr) into next 3 ch corner sp,

1 ch, (3 tr, into next 3 ch sp, 1 ch)
3 times; rep from * twice, join with sl
st into 3rd of 3 ch. Break off yarn D.
Round 7: Attach yarn A in any corner
3 ch sp with a sl st, 1 ch (1 dc, 3 ch,
1 dc) into same sp, 3 ch, (1 dc into
next 1 ch sp, 3 ch) 4 times, * (1 dc,
3 ch, 1 dc) into next 3 ch corner sp,
3 ch, (1 dc into next 1 ch sp, 3 ch)
4 times; rep from * twice, join with sl
st into first dc. Break off yarn A.

Continue increasing the square
in this manner using the colour
sequence:
B, A, C, A, B, A, D, A.

Work until you have 26 rounds
ending with a treble cluster round
in C.

Round 27: Attach yarn A to any
corner ch sp tbl, 2 ch (counts as
1 dc and 1 ch), 1 dc into same sp,
1 dc tbl in the top of every tr, and ch,
(1 dc tbl, 1 ch, 1 dc tbl) into each 3 ch
corner sp, join with sl st into 1 ch.
Round 28: Sl st to corner ch sp tbl,
1 ch, (1 dc tbl, 1 ch, 1 dc tbl) into
same sp, 1 dc tbl in the top of every
dc, (1 dc tbl, 1 ch, 1 dc tbl) into each
corner ch sp, join with sl st into 1 ch.
Fasten off and weave in all ends.

Zig-zag Blanket

There is something so restful about crocheting stripe patterns. This pattern has a little kick in it which brings an added interest. At first sight the colour sequence appears to be random and yet the key is to repeat the light cream colour on every sixth row; this little trick ensures a harmonious vintage look.

Finished size

The blanket is 31½in (80cm) wide and 39in (100cm) long.

You will need

- Stylecraft Special DK, 100% acrylic (322yd/295m) per 100g ball):
  1 x 1005 Cream (A)
  1 x 1825 Lobelia (B)
  1 x 1188 Lavender (C)
  1 x 1390 Clematis (D)
  1 x 1827 Fuchsia Purple (E)
  1 x 1823 Mustard (F)
  1 x 1065 Meadow (G)
  1 x 1725 Sage (H)
- 4mm (USG/6:UK8) crochet hook
- Tapestry needle

Tension

This is not essential for this pattern but each treble repeat is 4in (10cm) wide and there are 7 rows to each 4in (10cm).

Note

The colour sequence follows B, C, D, E, F, G, H, but ensure that you place a row of yarn A in every sixth row and then continue with the colour sequence.

Blanket

Row 1: Ch 164 sts, work 1 dc into 2nd ch, 1 dc in every ch to end, turn.
Row 2: Ch 1, 1 dc in each st to end, turn. Fasten off yarn A.
Row 3: Change to yarn B, 5 ch, 3 tr in dc at base of ch, miss 2 sts, *3 tr in next st, miss 2 sts, 3 tr in next st, miss 5 sts, 3 tr in next st, miss 2 sts, 3 tr in next st, miss 2 sts, (3 tr, 3 ch, 3 tr) in next st, miss 2 sts; rep from * eight times, 3 tr in next st, miss 2 sts, 3 tr in next st, miss 5 sts, 3 tr in next st, miss 2 sts, 3 tr in next st, miss 2 sts, (3 tr, 2 ch, 1 tr) in last st, turn. Fasten off yarn B.
Row 4 (Pattern Row): Change to yarn C, join with a sl st in the 2 ch sp on the previous row, 5 ch, 3 tr in same ch sp, * (miss 3 sts, 3 tr) twice, miss 6 sts, 3 tr, (miss 3 sts, 3 tr), miss 3 sts, (3 tr, 3 ch, 3 tr) in same 3 ch sp; rep from * 8 times, (miss 3 sts, 3 tr) twice, miss 6 sts, 3 tr, (miss 3 sts,

3 tr), miss 3 sts, (3 tr, 2 ch, 1 tr) in last 2 ch sp, turn. Break off yarn and fasten off.

Rep Row 4 using the colour sequence as a guide remembering that every 6th row is worked in yarn A. Ensure the last row 67 is worked in H.

Row 68: Change to yarn A, 1 ch, 2 dc in 2 ch sp, working into the top of each tr, * 8 dc, dc2tog, 8 dc, (1 dc, 1 ch, 1 dc) in 3 ch sp; rep from * 8 times, 8 dc, dc2tog, 8 dc, 2 dc in last ch sp, turn.
Row 69: Ch1, 2 dc in st at base of ch, working into the top of each st, * 8 dc, dc2tog, 8 dc, (1 dc, 1 ch, 1 dc) in ch sp; rep from * 8 times, 8 dc, dc2tog, 8 dc, 2 dc in last st.

Finishing

Fasten off and weave in all ends.

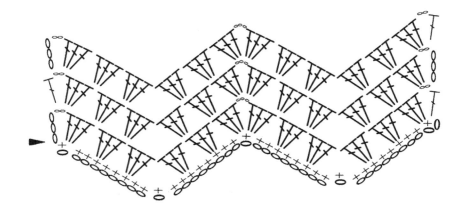

Four-square Blanket

I have a number of blankets that I keep permanently in our living room. When we want to get particularly cosy, we grab them and put them on our laps. The colours I have chosen for this design are unashamedly reminiscent of faded vintage cottage chic. You can expand this design to make a large throw for a bed, simply by multiplying the squares.

Finished size

The blanket is 38 x 38in (97 x 97cm) square.

You will need

- Stylecraft Special DK, 100% acrylic (322yd/295m) per 100g ball):
  2 x 1005 Cream (A)
  1 x 1842 Spearmint (B)
  1 x 1836 Vintage Peach (C)
  1 x 1712 Lime (D)
  1 x 1026 Apricot (E)
- 4mm (USG/6:UK8) crochet hook
- Tapestry needle

Tension

This is not essential for this pattern but each square motif is approximately 19 x 19in (48 x 48cm).

Note

You will need to make four square motifs for this design. I have chosen five colours and, ideally, to get that vintage look you change the order of the colours. However, make sure rounds 8–10 and round 20 are always worked in yarn A. Rounds 2–4 and rounds 17–19 should always be the same colour.

Basic square

Round 1: Using 4mm hook and B, ch 6 sts, join with a sl st to form a ring.

Round 2: Ch 6 (this counts as the first tr and 3 ch), (3 tr into ring, 3 ch) 3 times, 2 tr into ring, sl st into 3rd of 6 ch at the beg of round.

Round 3: Slip st into corner ch sp, 6 ch (counts as the first tr and 3 ch), 3 tr into same ch sp, *1 ch, miss 3 tr, (3 tr, 3 ch, 3 tr) into next ch sp; rep from * twice, 1 ch, miss 3 tr, 2 tr into next ch sp, sl st into 3rd of 6 ch at beg of round.

Round 4: Slip st into corner ch sp, 6 ch (counts as the first tr and 3 ch), 3 tr into same ch sp, *1 ch, miss 3 tr, 3 tr into next ch sp, 1 ch, miss 3 tr, (3 tr, 3 ch, 3 tr) into next ch sp; rep from * twice, 1 ch, miss 3 tr, 3 tr into next ch sp, 1 ch, miss 3 tr, 2 tr into next ch sp, sl st into 3rd of 6 ch at beg of round. Fasten off.

Round 5: Attach yarn C in any corner chain sp with a sl st, 6 ch (counts as the first tr and 3 ch), 3 tr into same ch sp, *(1 ch, miss 3 tr, 3 tr into next ch sp) twice, 1 ch, miss 3 tr, (3 tr, 3 ch, 3 tr) into next ch sp; rep from * twice, (1 ch, miss 3 tr, 3 tr into next ch sp) twice, 1 ch, miss 3 tr, 2 tr into next ch sp, sl st into 3rd of 6 ch at beg of round.

Round 6: Slip st into corner ch sp, 6 ch (counts as the first tr and 3 ch), 3 tr into same ch sp, *(1 ch, miss 3 tr, 3 tr into next ch sp) 3 times, 1 ch, miss 3 tr, (3 tr, 3 ch, 3 tr) into next ch sp; rep from * twice, (1 ch, miss 3 tr, 3 tr into next ch sp) 3 times, 1 ch, miss 3 tr, 2 tr into next ch sp, sl st into 3rd of 6 ch at beg of round.

Round 7: Slip st into corner ch sp, 6 ch (counts as the first tr and 3 ch), 3 tr into same ch sp, *(1 ch, miss 3 tr, 3 tr into next ch sp) 4 times, 1 ch, miss 3 tr, (3 tr, 3 ch, 3 tr) into next ch sp; rep from * twice, (1 ch, miss 3 tr, 3 tr into next ch sp) 4 times, 1 ch, miss 3 tr, 2 tr into next ch sp, sl st into 3rd of 6 ch at beg of round. Fasten off.

Round 8: Attach yarn A in any corner chain sp with a sl st, 6 ch (counts as the first tr and 3 ch), 3 tr into same ch sp, *(1 ch, miss 3 tr, 3 tr into next ch sp) 5 times, 1 ch, miss 3 tr, (3 tr, 3 ch, 3 tr) into next ch sp; rep from * twice, (1 ch, miss 3 tr, 3 tr into next ch sp) 5 times, 1 ch, miss 3 tr, 2 tr into next ch sp, sl st into 3rd of 6 ch at beg of round.

Continue increasing the granny square in this manner, working three rounds in each colour.

Rounds 9–10: Work in yarn A.
Rounds 11–13: Work in yarn D.
Rounds 14–16: Work in yarn E.
Rounds 17–19: Work in yarn B.
Round 20: Work in yarn A.

Make a further three squares using the following colour combinations:

Square 2

Rounds 2–4: Work in yarn D.
Rounds 5–7: Work in yarn E.
Rounds 8–10: Work in yarn A.
Rounds 11–13: Work in yarn B
Rounds 14–16: Work in yarn C.
Rounds 17–19: Work in yarn D.
Round 20: Work in yarn A.

Square 3

Rounds 2–4: Work in yarn E.
Rounds 5–7: Work in yarn B.
Rounds 8–10: Work in yarn A.
Rounds 11–13: Work in yarn C
Rounds 14–16: Work in yarn D.
Rounds 17–19: Work in yarn E.
Round 20: Work in yarn A.

Square 4

Rounds 2–4: Work in yarn C.
Rounds 5–7: Work in yarn D.
Rounds 9–10: Work in yarn A.
Rounds 11–13: Work in yarn E
Rounds 14–16: Work in yarn B.
Rounds 17–19: Work in yarn C.
Round 20: Work in yarn A.

Finishing

Weave in ends. Arrange your squares in 2 rows of 2 squares. Join the squares together using yarn A, by placing a sl st in the back loop of each st in each square. Work horizontally first and then work vertically. Weave in all ends.

Edging

Join E to any corner of the blanket with a sl st.

Round 1: Attach yarn E to any corner ch sp tbl, 2 ch (counts as 1 dc and 1 ch), 1 dc into same sp, 1 dc tbl in the top of every tr, ch and seam edge, (1 dc tbl, 1 ch, 1 dc tbl) into each 3 ch corner sp, join with sl st into 1 ch. Fasten off.

Round 2: Attach yarn C to any corner ch sp tbl, 4 ch (counts as 1 htr and 2 ch), 1 htr tbl into same sp, 1 htr tbl in the top of every dc, (1 htr tbl, 2 ch, 1 htr tbl) into each corner ch sp, join with sl st into 2 ch. Fasten off and weave in all ends.

Cocoon Shrug

The weekend should be about wearing comfy and snuggly clothing. Feet up on the sofa with the softest crochet around your shoulders. This stylish shrug will become your go-to friend for relaxing by the fire and is made simply out of a large granny square.

Finished size

Finished square is 39in (100cm). If you want to make your shrug smaller or larger, measure the space from one elbow, across your shoulders to the other elbow. Make the finished square this size before attaching the sleeves and creating the collar and cuff.

You will need

- Scheepjes Scrumptious DK, 50% polyester, 50% acrylic (328yd/300m per 100g ball):
  2 x 100g 311 Chai Shortbread (A)
  1 x 100g 330 Cotton Candy Meringue (B)
  1 x 100g 308 Grapefruit Curd Tart (C)
  1 x 100g 324 Huckleberry Pie (D)
  1 x 100g 303 Green Velvet Cake (E)
  1 x 100g 328 Ocean Pudding Cup (F)
  1 x 100g 314 Blue Glazed Doughnut (G)
- 3.5mm (USE/4:UK9) crochet hook
- Tapestry needle

Tension

This is not essential for this pattern.

Note

The shrug is created by making a large granny square which you then join to create armholes and the collar.

Shrug

Round 1: Using 3.5mm hook and B, ch 4 sts, join with a sl st to form a ring.

Round 2: Ch 6 (this counts as the first tr and 3 ch), (3 tr into ring, 3 ch) 3 times, 2 tr into ring, sl st into 3rd of 6 ch at the beg of round. Fasten off.

Round 3: Attach yarn A in any 2 ch sp with a sl st, 1 ch, (1 dc, 3 ch, 1 dc) into same sp, 3 ch, * (1 dc, 3 ch, 1 dc) into next ch sp, 3 ch; rep from * twice, join with sl st to first dc. Fasten off.

Round 4: Attach C in any corner chain sp with a sl st, 6 ch (counts as the first tr and 3 ch), 3 tr into same ch sp, *1 ch, 3 tr into next 3 ch sp, 1 ch, (3 tr, 3 ch, 3 tr) into next ch sp; rep from * twice, 1 ch, 3 tr into next 3 ch sp, 1 ch, 2 tr into next ch sp, sl st into 3rd of 6 ch at beg of round. Fasten off.

Round 5: Attach yarn A in any corner 3 ch sp with a sl st, 1 ch (1 dc, 3 ch, 1 dc) into same sp, 3 ch, (1 dc into next 1 ch sp, 3 ch) twice, * (1 dc, 3 ch, 1 dc) into next 3 ch corner sp, 3 ch, (1 dc into next 1 ch sp, 3 ch) twice; rep from * twice, join with sl st into first dc. Fasten off.

Round 6: Attach D in any corner chain sp with a sl st, 6 ch (counts as the first tr and 3 ch), 3 tr into same ch sp, *(1 ch, 3 tr into next 3 ch sp) three times, 1 ch, (3 tr, 3 ch, 3 tr) into next ch sp; rep from * twice, (1 ch, 3 tr into next 3 ch sp) three times, 1 ch, 2 tr into next ch sp, sl st into 3rd of 6 ch at beg of round. Fasten off.

Round 7: Attach yarn A in any corner 3 ch sp with a sl st, 1 ch (1 dc, 3 ch, 1 dc) into same sp, 3 ch, (1 dc into next 1 ch sp, 3 ch) 4 times, * (1 dc, 3 ch, 1 dc) into next 3 ch corner sp, 3 ch, (1 dc into next 1 ch sp, 3 ch) 4 times; rep from * twice, join with sl st into first dc. Fasten off.

Continue increasing the granny square in this manner using the colour sequence:

E, A, F, A, G, A, B, A, C, A, D, A

Work until you have 196 treble clusters ending with a row in B.

Finishing

Fold your square in half to form a rectangle, with the 'wrong' side facing out. Sew up one of the short sides (or use a dc or sl st join), stopping about 18cm (7in) before the fold to form the armholes. Fasten off.

Sleeve cuffs

Round 1: With RS facing using 3.5mm hook, join B to the seam of the armhole 3 ch, 1 tr into each tr, sl st into 3rd ch.

Rounds 2–4: Ch 2, *1 rtrf in next st, 1 rtrb in next st; rep from * to one from end, sl st into 3rd ch. Fasten off and weave in ends.

Collar

Round 1: With RS facing using 3.5mm hook, join B to the top of any treble, 3 ch, 1 tr into each tr, and 1 tr in the top of each seam, sl st into 3rd ch, turn.

Rounds 2–4: Ch 2, *1 rtrf in next st, 1 rtrb in next st; rep from * to one from end, sl st into 3rd ch. Fasten off and weave in ends.

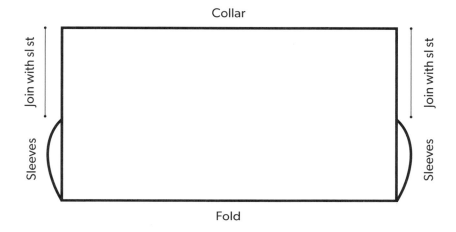

Patchwork Star Blanket

When you learn how to work half-and-half granny squares a world of new pattern combinations is opened up to you. I love this traditional quilt star pattern and although I don't have the skills of a quilter, I can create a similar homely effect using crochet squares.

Finished size

Finished blanket is approximately 48 x 48in (122 x 122cm)

You will need

- Stylecraft Special Aran, 100% acrylic (214yd/196m per 100g ball):
  5 x 1005 Cream (A)
- Stylecraft Batik DK, 20% wool, 80% acrylic (150yd/138m) per 100g ball):
  2 x 1914 Indigo (B)
  2 x 1913 Storm (C)
  1 x 1916 Rose (D)
- 3.5mm (USE/4:UK9) crochet hook
- Tapestry needle

Tension

This is not essential for this pattern but each square motif is approximately 3½ x 3½in (9 x 9cm).

Note

Make 196 squares, put together in rows of 14 x 14.

When working the half-and-half squares refer to diagram to understand where each st is placed.

Make 100 plain squares with yarn A, 4 with yarn B and 4 with yarn C. Make 32 half-and-half squares with yarns A & B, 32 with yarns A & C, 16 with yarns A & D and 8 with yarns B & C.

Plain square

Using 3.5mm hook and A, ch 4 sts, join with a sl st to form a ring.

Round 1: Ch 5 (this counts as 1 tr, 2 ch), 3 tr into ring, *2 ch, 3 tr; rep from * twice, 2 ch, 2 tr, sl st into 3rd ch at the beg of round (4 tr clusters). Do not fasten off.

Round 2: Sl st into 2 ch sp, 3 ch (counts as 1 tr), (1 tr, 2 ch, 2 tr) into same ch sp, *1 tr into each tr across side of square, (2 tr, 2 ch, 2 tr) into next 2 ch sp; rep from * twice, 1 tr in each tr across side of square, join with a sl st into 3rd of 3 ch.

Round 3: Sl st into 2 ch sp, 3 ch (counts as 1 tr), (1 tr, 2 ch, 2 tr) into same ch sp, *1 tr into each tr across side of square, (2 tr, 2 ch, 2 tr) into next 2 ch sp; rep from * twice, 1 tr in each tr across side of square, join with a sl st into 3rd of 3 ch.

Half-and-half square

Using 3.5mm hook and A (or first shade), ch 4 sts, join with a sl st to form a ring.

Round 1: Ch 3 (this counts as 1 tr on this and following rounds), (2 tr, 2 ch, 3 tr) into ring, 1 ch, join in second shade (do not fasten off), 1 ch, (3 tr, 2 ch, 3 tr), 2 ch, sl st to join, turn.

Round 2: Sl st into corner ch sp, 3 ch, 1 tr into same corner ch sp, 3 tr, (2 tr, 2 ch, 2 tr) into next 3 ch sp, 3 tr, 2 tr in next corner ch sp, 1 ch, change to first shade, drop second shade ready to pick up on next rnd, (do not work over it), 1 ch, 2 tr in same corner sp, 3 tr, (2 tr, 2 ch, 2 tr) in next corner ch sp, 3 tr, 2 tr in first corner 2 ch sp, 2 ch, sl st in third of beg 3 ch to join, turn.

Round 3: Sl st into corner ch sp, 3 ch, 1 tr into same corner ch sp, 1 tr in each tr to next corner ch sp, (2 tr, 2 ch, 2 tr) into next 2 ch sp, 1 tr in each tr to next corner ch sp, 2 tr in next corner ch sp, 1 ch, change yarn dropping yarn, 1 ch, 2 tr in same corner sp, 1 tr in each tr to next corner ch sp, (2 tr, 2 ch, 2 tr) in next corner ch sp, 1 tr in each tr to first 2 ch sp, 2 tr in first corner 2 ch sp, 2 ch, sl st in third of beg 3 ch to join, Fasten off and weave in all ends.

Finishing

Block your squares to create neat corners and edging.
Arrange squares to match arrangement on diagram.
Using yarn A and with WS facing, join the motifs from the back by working rows of dc stitches vertically and then horizontally.
Work 1 dc in each corner ch sp and 1 dc in top of each side st.

Edging

Round 1: With RS facing, join yarn A with a sl st 7 sts in from the corner of the blanket, 1 ch, 1 dc in base of ch, 1 dc in the top of each st, 1 dc in each ch sp, 1 dc in the top of each seam around, working (1 dc, 2 ch, 1 dc) in each corner ch sp, join with sl st to first ch.

Round 2: With RS facing, join yarn B with a sl st to any dc st on prev rnd, 2 ch, work 1 htr in each dc and (1 htr, 2 ch, 1 htr) in each corner ch sp around, join with sl st to first ch.
Fasten off and weave in all ends.

Beautiful Vintage Blanket

This blanket is the very essence of vintage crochet. You might find a similar pattern made from the 1940s and 50s, but many people have snapped up these heirloom treasures. So the only thing for it is to make your own. I have given you the yarn shades I have used, but really if you have a stash of yarn, this is the perfect design to use up those odds and ends.

Finished size

The blanket is 72 x 72in (183 x 183cm) square.

You will need

- Stylecraft Special DK, 100% acrylic (322yd/295m per 100g ball):
  7 x 1005 Cream (A)
  1 x 1842 Spearmint (B)
  1 x 1843 Powder Pink (C)
  1 x 1711 Spice (D)
  1 x 1823 Mustard (E)
  1 x 1302 Denim (F)
  1 x 1019 Cloud Blue (G)
  1 x 1725 Sage (H)
  1 x 1724 Parma Violet (I)
  1 x 1123 Claret (J)
  1 x 1390 Clematis (K)
  1 x 1827 Fuchsia Purple (L)
  1 x 1854 French Navy (M)
  1 x 1852 Apple (N)
- 3.5mm (USE/4:UK9) crochet hook
- Tapestry needle

Tension

This is not essential for this pattern but each square motif is approximately 19 x 19in (48 x 48cm).

Note

This blanket is made up of square sections – it is four large squares wide by six large squares long. Each square pattern is made up of nine assorted granny squares all edged with a zesty spearmint shade and the background and edging is in cream.

I have added a lacy chain stitch border.

For the granny squares, use the photograph as a guide and combine lots of different colours but ensure that round 4 is always in yarn A. Do not use yarn B in any of your individual granny squares.

Basic square

Round 1: Using 3.5mm hook and C, ch 6 sts, join with a sl st to form a ring.
Round 2: Ch 6 (this counts as the first tr and 3 ch), (3 tr into ring, 3 ch) 3 times, 2 tr into ring, sl st into 3rd of 6 ch at the beg of round. Fasten off.
Round 3: Attach yarn D into corner ch sp, 6 ch (counts as the first tr and 3 ch), 3 tr into same ch sp, *1 ch, miss 3 tr, (3 tr, 3 ch, 3 tr) into next ch sp; rep from * twice, 1 ch, miss 3 tr, 2 tr into next ch sp, sl st into 3rd of 6 ch at beg of round. Fasten off.
Round 4: Attach yarn A into corner ch sp, 6 ch (counts as the first tr and 3 ch), 3 tr into same ch sp, *1 ch, miss 3 tr, 3 tr into next ch sp, 1 ch, miss 3 tr, (3 tr, 3 ch, 3 tr) into next ch sp; rep from * twice, 1 ch, miss 3 tr, 3 tr into next ch sp, 1 ch, miss 3 tr, 2 tr into next ch sp, sl st into 3rd of 6 ch at beg of round. Fasten off.

You can complete all your squares in this way and sew the edges together

for the 3 x 3 granny square motif. However, you can also join your granny squares as you go.

Second square – join as you go

Round 4: Attach yarn in any corner chain sp, 6 ch (counts as the first tr and 3 ch), 3 tr into same ch sp, (1 ch, miss 3 tr, 3 tr into next ch sp), 1 ch, 3 tr in next ch sp, 1 ch, dc into any 3 ch corner sp of first square, 1 ch, then work 3 tr in second square corner ch sp, (1 ch, dc into next 1 ch sp of first square, 3 tr in next 1 ch sp of the second square), 1 ch, 3 tr in next 3 ch sp of round 3 of the second square, 1 ch, dc into 3 ch corner sp of first square, 1 ch, 3 tr in second square corner ch sp.
Finish off second square as normal granny round: (1 ch, 3 tr into next ch sp), 1 ch, (3 tr, 3 ch, 3 tr) into next ch sp, (1 ch, 3 tr into next ch sp), 1 ch, miss 3 tr, 2 tr into next ch sp, sl st into 3rd of 6 ch at beg of round. Fasten off.

Two squares have been joined. Join the next squares like this until a row of eight squares has been completed.

Second row and following rows. Join the first square of the next row to the bottom of the first square of the previous row.

Second square of second row can be attached to the blanket along two sides. This will be true of the following rows.

Round 4: Attach yarn in any corner chain sp, 6 ch (counts as the first tr and 3 ch), 3 tr into same ch sp, (1 ch, 3 tr into next ch sp), 1 ch, 3 tr in next ch sp, 1 ch, dc into any 3 ch corner sp of first square, 1 ch, then work 3 tr in working square corner ch sp, (1 ch, dc into next 1 ch sp of first square, 3 tr in next 1 ch sp of round 3 of the working square), 1 ch, 3 tr in next 3 ch sp of round 3 of the working square, 1 ch, dc into 3 ch corner sp of first square, 1 ch, 3 tr in working square corner ch sp, (1 ch, dc into next 1 ch sp of square above, 3 tr in next 1 ch sp of round 3 of the working square), 1 ch, 3 tr in next 3 ch sp of round 3 of the working square, 1 ch, dc into 3 ch corner sp of square above, 1 ch, 3 tr in working square corner ch sp.
Finish off working square as normal: (1 ch, 3 tr into next ch sp), 1 ch, 2 tr into next ch sp, sl st into 3rd of 6 ch at beg of round. Fasten off.

Continue to join squares like this along two sides until you have three rows, three squares wide. Work until your blanket is eight squares by eight squares.

Granny stripe edges

Starting with yarn B, work 3 rows of granny square clusters around the outside of the 9 granny square motifs.

Round 1: Using 3.5mm hook and B, attach yarn to a 3 ch corner sp at one end of the corner of the joined squares, 3 ch (counts as the first tr), (2 tr, 3 ch, 3 tr) into sp, *(1 ch, 3 tr in next ch sp) twice, 1 ch, 3 tr in between granny squares; rep from * once, (1 ch, 3 tr in next ch sp) twice, 1 ch, (3 tr, 3 ch, 3 tr) in the 3 ch corner sp, work in this way around the edge of the 3 x 3 granny squares, 1 ch, join with a sl st into 3rd of 3 ch. Fasten off.
Rounds 2–3: Join yarn A to a 3 ch corner sp of the joined squares, 3 ch (counts as the first tr), (2 tr, 3 ch, 3 tr) into sp, (1 ch, 3 tr in next 1 ch sp) around, working (3 tr, 3 ch, 3 tr) in the 3 ch corners, 1 ch join with a sl st into 3rd of 3 ch.

Use the join as you go method to attach the large granny square motifs together on round 3 using yarn A. Make sure that your blanket is 4 large granny square motifs wide and 6 motifs long.

Blanket edges

Round 1: Using 3.5mm hook and A, attach yarn to a 3 ch corner sp at one end of the corner of the long side of the joined squares, 3 ch (counts as the first tr), (2 tr, 3 ch, 3 tr) into sp, *(1 ch, 3 tr in next ch sp) 11 times, 1 ch, 3 tr in between granny squares; rep from * 4 times, (1 ch, 3 tr in next ch sp) 11 times, 1 ch, (3 tr, 3 ch, 3 tr) in the 3 ch corner sp, work in this way around the edge of the 4 x 6 granny squares, 1 ch, join with a sl st into 3rd of 3 ch.
Rounds 2–4: Sl st into corner ch sp, 3 ch, dc in same space, *3 ch, miss 1 tr, 1 dc in next tr, 3 ch, miss 1 tr, 1 dc in ch sp; rep from * around, work (1 dc, 3 ch, 1 dc) into 3 ch corner sp, join with a sl st to base of first ch.
Using a tapestry needle, weave in all the ends.

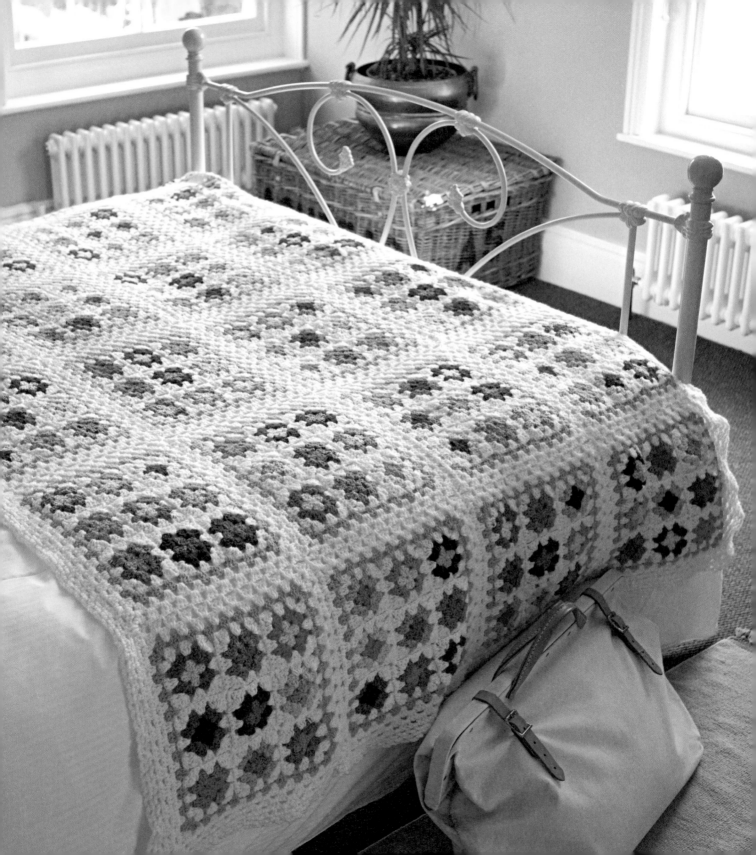

Soft Summer Blanket

This pretty blanket simply evolved. I started making squares that were inspired by the colours I saw in my garden. It just grew and grew and in the end I made a blanket big enough for a British single bed or as a generous footer at the base of a king-size bed.

Finished size

The blanket is 50in (127cm) wide and 70in (180cm) long.

You will need

- Stylecraft Special DK, 100% acrylic (322yd/295m per 100g ball):
  2 x 1080 Pale Rose (A)
  2 x 1005 Cream (B)
  2 x 1725 Sage (C)
  2 x 1823 Mustard (D)
  2 x 1302 Denim (E)
  2 x 1023 Raspberry (F)
  2 x 1019 Cloud Blue (G)
- 3.5mm (USE/4:UK9) crochet hook
- Tapestry needle

Tension

This is not essential for this pattern but each square motif is approximately 5½ x 5½in (14 x 14cm).

Note

Make 36 granny squares which have 6 rows. Make rows 1–5 in different colours and try to make sure there is an equal distribution of colours. Don't use pale rose (A) in rows 1–5 but use it for Row 6 (the last row) for each square.

Basic granny square

Round 1: Using 3.5mm hook and F, ch 4 sts, sl st in first ch to form a loop.

Round 2: 3 ch, 2 tr in loop, 3 ch, (3 tr, 3 ch) rep twice more, sl st in 3 ch (4 tr clusters).

Round 3: Change to B, attach yarn to any 3 ch sp, (3 ch, 2 tr, 3 ch, 3 tr, 1 ch) in ch sp, (3 tr, 3 ch, 3 tr, 1 ch) in next ch sp, 3 times, sl st in 3 ch (8 tr clusters).

Round 4: Change to C, attach yarn to any 3 ch sp, (3 ch, 2 tr, 3 ch, 3 tr, 1 ch) in ch sp, (3 tr, 1 ch) in next ch sp, *(3 tr, 3 ch, 3 tr, 1 ch) in next 3 ch sp, (3 tr, 1 ch) in next ch sp; rep from * twice more, sl st in 3 ch (12 tr clusters).

Round 5: Change to D, attach yarn to any 3 ch sp, (3 ch, 2 tr, 3 ch, 3 tr, 1 ch) in ch sp, (3 tr, 1 ch) in next 2 ch sps, *(3 tr, 3 ch, 3 tr, 1 ch) in next 3 ch sp, (3 tr, 1 ch) in next 2 ch sps; rep from * twice more, sl st in 3 ch (16 tr clusters).

Round 6: Change to E, attach yarn to any 3 ch sp, (3 ch, 2 tr, 3 ch, 3 tr, 1 ch) in ch sp, (3 tr, 1 ch) in next 3 ch sps, *(3 tr, 3 ch, 3 tr, 1 ch) in next 3 ch sp, (3 tr, 1 ch) in next 3 ch sps; rep from * twice more, sl st in 3 ch (20 tr clusters).

Round 7: Change to A, attach yarn to any 3 ch sp, (3 ch, 2 tr, 3 ch, 3 tr, 1 ch) in ch sp, (3 tr, 1 ch) in next 4 ch sps, *(3 tr, 3 ch, 3 tr, 1 ch) in next 3 ch sp, (3 tr, 1 ch) in next 4 ch sps; rep from * twice more, sl st in 3 ch (24 tr clusters).

Fasten off and weave in ends.

I blocked each square at this stage as I find it helps with accurately joining each square together. Using yarn A, I slip-stitched the squares together to make a 6 x 6 square.

Granny stripe edges

I then worked 16 rows of granny square clusters around the outside of the 36 squares. Each row was a different colour – however, the 2nd row, and following 2 x 5th rows, were cream.

Round 1: Using 3.5mm hook and D, attach yarn to a 3 ch corner sp at one end of the corner of the large joined squares, 3 ch (counts as the first tr), (2 tr, 3 ch, 3 tr) into sp, *(1 ch, 3 tr in next ch sp), rep around the edge of the joined square, working (3 tr, 3 ch, 3 tr) in the 3 ch corner sps, 1 ch, join with a sl st into 3rd of 3 ch. Fasten off.

Round 2: Join yarn B to a 3 ch corner sp, 3 ch (counts as the first tr), (2 tr, 3 ch, 3 tr) into sp, (1 ch, 3 tr in next 1 ch sp) around, working (3 tr, 3 ch, 3 tr) in the 3 ch corners, 1 ch, join with a sl st into 3rd of 3 ch.

Rounds 3–16: Rep round 2 using the colour sequence: G, E, A, D, B, F, G, E, A, B, D, F, G, E.

Add more single rows to each end of the blanket to turn it from being a square into a rectangle. Starting with a cream row, I added 14 more rows. The first and every following 5th row was cream. I repeated the colour striping on the other side of the blanket.

Row 1: Using 3.5mm hook and B, attach yarn to a 3 ch corner sp at one end of the corner of the large joined squares, 3 ch (counts as the first tr), 1 tr in same sp, (1 ch, 3 tr in next ch sp), rep to end, 1 ch, 2 tr in the 3 ch corner sp, turn. Fasten off.

Row 2: Attach yarn A to top of 3 ch, 4 ch (counts as first tr and 1 ch), 3 tr in next ch sp, (1 ch, 3 tr in next 1 ch sp) rep to end, 1 tr in turning ch of previous row, turn. Fasten off.

Row 3: Attach yarn D to top of 3 ch, 3 ch, 1 tr in ch sp at base of ch, (1 ch, 3 tr in next 1 ch sp), rep to end, 2 tr in last ch sp of previous row, turn. Fasten off.

Rows 4–16: Rep rows 2–3 using colour sequence: F, G, B, E, A, D, F, B, G, E, A, D.

Edging

You will finally work a linen stitch edging.

Round 1: With RS facing, using 3.5mm hook attach yarn B to the top of any treble, 1 ch, 1 dc into each tr and ch st, 2 dc in the sides of any tr st around, work (1 dc, 1 ch, 1 dc) into each corner, 1 ch, sl st into first ch. Fasten off.

Now you will work 3 rounds of linen stitch using the colour sequence: F, A, E.

Rounds 2–4: With RS facing, attach yarn, 2 ch, miss 1 dc at base of ch, (1 dc in next st, 1 ch, miss 1 st), rep around, work (1 dc, 1 ch, 1 dc) in each corner, 1 ch, sl st in first ch. Fasten off and weave in ends.

Finishing

Weave in all ends.

Handy tip

If you find that the edges of your blankets go wavy and frilled instead of flat, try using a hook one size smaller than you used for the squares.

Resources

Suppliers

The yarn used in these projects should be available from your local yarn or craft store. If you can't find them, try one of the websites listed below.

UK

Black Sheep Wools
blacksheepwools.com

Debbie Bliss Designer Yarns
debbieblissonline.com

Fred Aldous: Art & Craft Supplies
fredaldous.co.uk

Hobbycraft
hobbycraft.co.uk

Stylecraft
stylecraft-yarns.co.uk

USA

Hobby Lobby
hobbylobby.com

LoveCrafts
lovecrafts.com/en-us

Michaels
michaels.com

Acknowledgements

Working on the book is a team effort. Lots of talented people think about the projects, the patterns and the images so that your experience is good. I would like to thank the wonderful team at GMC, especially my editor Sara who is very patient. Thank you also to Jonathan Bailey, the publisher who trusts me to come up with appealing projects. Thanks must also go to the wonderful photographer, Andrew Perris, the stylist, Anna Stevens and to Robin Shields for the overall design. Thank you also to Jude Roust, who did a wonderful job checking the patterns.

I would like to thank a number of yarn producers and retailers for their support; Thanks to Stylecraft Ltd and the team at Spa Mill, Annabell and Juliet, who generously donated many of the yarns for the blankets.

I am grateful to my family, who always encourage me to create and put up with so much yarn in our lives. For this book Benjamin and Robert have been my quality controllers and my time-keepers – I love you and thank you for your cheerleading.

Index

First published 2024 by
Guild of Master Craftsman Publications Ltd, Castle Place, 166 High Street, Lewes, East Sussex,
BN7 1XU, UK

Text © Emma Varnam, 2024
Copyright in the Work © GMC Publications Ltd, 2024

ISBN 978 1 78494 679 1

Publisher Jonathan Bailey
Production Jim Bulley
Senior Project Editor Sara Harper
Design Manager Robin Shields
Stylist Anna Stevens
Photographer Andrew Perris
Technical illustrators Simon Rodway, Martin Woodward

Colour origination by GMC Reprographics
Printed and bound in China

To order a book, or to request
a catalogue, contact:
GMC Publications Ltd
Castle Place, 166 High Street, Lewes,
East Sussex, BN7 1XU
United Kingdom
Tel: +44 (0)1273 488005
www.gmcbooks.com